P9-AQF-795

※※

Was Never Here and
This Never Happened

※※

I Was Never Here and This Never Happened

Tasty Bits & Spicy Tales
from My Life

Dorinda Hafner

1↺
TEN SPEED PRESS
Berkeley, California

A Kirsty Melville Book

1☺
Ten Speed Press
P.O. Box 7123
Berkeley, California 94707

Distributed in Australia by E. J. Dwyer Pty. Ltd., in Canada by Publishers Group
West, in New Zealand by Tandem Press, in South Africa by Real Books, and in the
United Kingdom and Europe by Airlift Books.

Cover and interior design by Nancy Austin.
Map by Akiko Shurtleff.

Library of Congress Cataloging-in-Publication Data
    Hafner, Dorinda.
        I Was Never Here & This Never Happened
            p.   cm
        ISBN 0-89815-641-6 (pbk.)
            1. Folklore—Ghana   2. Food habits—Ghana   3. Cookery, Ghanaian.
    4. Ghana—Social life and customs. I. Title.
    GR351.6.H34   1995
    398'.09667—dc20   95-16704
                                                                        CIP

First printing, 1996
Printed in Singapore

1 2 3 4 5 6 7 8 9 10 — 00 99 98 97 96

Dedicated to my mother
Elizabeth Naa Lamiley Bannerman-Addy

and my father
Ayitey Kojo Addy, alias Naatse or A.K.

and my dear Aunty Awuraba
Beatrice Betty Bannerman

The fires that melted my butter and coddled my eggs!

BURKINA FASO

BENIN

TOGO

IVORY COAST

Volta River

Oti River

Lake Volta

Mmofraturo Girls School

Kumasi

Nkawkaw

Kibi

ACCRA

Wesley Girls High School

Tarkwa

Cape Coast

ATLANTIC OCEAN

0   100 km

0   100 miles

GHANA

Acknowledgments

Phil Wood   the visionary, for taking a gamble on me.

Kirsty Melville   my publisher, for your support and unshakable faith.

Mariah Bear   my "needle in a haystack" editor. You are a gem!

Clancy Drake   of the "Never-Never," thanks for refusing to accept "I can't" as an answer.

Lisa Zuré Ruffin   for traversing across the world to access my stories, and for your unorthodox methods and madness, thanks.

Nancy Austin   for your beautiful design and layout.

Donna Latte   for hours of proofreading and typing.

Akiko Shurtleff   for your cartography.

Kwame Asumadu, Seth Annang, my children James and Nvala, my dear friends Barb Allert, Mary McMinn, and many other friends whose encouragement kept the flame within me alive to continue writing.

Me da mo ase pii
Mii da nyeshi waa

(Top line means "Thank you very much" in Ashanti)
(Second line means "I thank you very much" in Ga)

Contents

Who I Am and
Why I'm Writing This Book

"It is imperative that a woman keep her sense of humor intact
and at the ready. She must see, even if only in secret, that
she is the funniest, looniest woman in her world, which she
should also see as being the most absurd world of all times."

—MAYA ANGELOU

Being a black woman in a place like Adelaide, Australia can
be trying. Almost every single day somebody comes up to
me and says, "Where are you from?" So I answer, "I'm from
Ghana, in West Africa." They say, "How long have you been here? Do
you like Australia? What are you doing here?" and I go through the
whole routine, answering all their questions politely and then say
good-bye. After so many years of living here it has become quite
dreary, especially when it happens several times during the same trip
to the supermarket.

I turn the frozen foods aisle and somebody asks, "Where are you
from?" I answer them. I turn down by the drinks. "Where are you
from?" And I answer them. I turn down the detergents aisle. "Where

are you from?" I answer again. I turn and head for the breakfast cereal...and so on. By the time I get to the checkout stand, if anybody else asks, "Where are you from?" I'm ready to scream.

One particular evening, I hurried into the supermarket thinking, *God I hope nobody asks where I'm from today. I've got fifteen minutes to get in and out of here.*

I stood before the veal, neatly arranged in polystyrene trays, thinking how much healthier the meal would be if I used chicken fillets, because there would be less fat. It was bad enough that I had to use whole cream in the sauce. Just as I was about to move off, a hand descended on my shoulder, followed by a dainty voice.

"Hello, where are you from?"

I closed my eyes and gritted my teeth—*Oh God, not again.* Rather aggressively, I turned around, ready to pounce on whoever it was, and found myself face to face with a little old lady with blue-rinsed hair. Neatly dressed, the establishment type.

"Where are you from?"

I took a deep breath. My culture had a hold on me in a way that I wasn't even aware of until recently. You see, I had been brought up to respect the older generation, so I answered her, "I'm from Ghana, West Africa."

"Oh. How long have you been here?"

"I live here."

She ignored that and asked, "Do you like it in Australia?"

I thought, *Of course I like it you silly old bag, I wouldn't be here if I didn't.* But naturally, what you think and what comes out of your mouth are two different things, and so I answered, "Yes, I like it here, very much."

"So, when are you going back?"

I paused, looked her up and down, and replied, "I haven't actually thought about it."

"Oh. Do you shop a lot in this supermarket?"

"Yes."

"What are you getting today?"

What a nosy woman. But still I answered politely, "I was going to cook veal cordon bleu for my children but..."

"Oh," she said. "You do eat meat? So, what sort of meat do you eat where you come from?"

Well, maybe all was not lost. I could at least take a moment to educate this woman. I quickly went through the whole thing about how West Africans, being from the Atlantic coast, were largely fish eaters and not meat eaters, and how when we do eat meat we eat good meat—lamb, goat, or occasionally pork or locally bred poultry for special occasions. She seemed satisfied with my answer and I was glad to have taught her a little something.

"Well, good-bye," she said, "I hope you enjoy your stay."

As she walked away, I thought, *Oh God, the poor old dear can't be very bright, I've just told her I live here.*

I'd just moved on to the chicken section and was standing there, examining the fillets, when another hand descended on my shoulder. I thought I really would snap. I turned around....

It was the same old woman. This time, she came conspiratorially close to me and said, "I suppose you must miss your real sort of meat?"

Hadn't I just explained to this woman a few seconds ago what sort of meat and fish we ate? Why was she doing this to me? She moved even closer and before I could answer, she whispered, "I believe the missionaries put a stop to it in Papua, New Guinea, but I hear they still practice it in the highlands. You poor love, you must miss your real sort of meat!"

I was absolutely floored. For the first time it dawned on me that the woman might not be all there. Indeed, she seemed to be two sheep short in the top paddock. I felt a twinge of guilt for having had such mean thoughts about her, so I tried to be extra polite. "No, actually we do eat lamb and beef, same as..."

She cut me off mid sentence and said more insistently, "You must really miss your real sort of meat, I know."

Well, I looked at this frail, blue-rinsed old woman, her little lily-white arms sticking out from her short-sleeved blouse, and thought, *Why disappoint her?* I grabbed the arm closest to me, took a deep breath and sunk my mouth onto her forearm, which I sucked and pretended to bite.

The woman shrieked, "She bit me! She bit me!"

Her shriek drew attention from the other shoppers. Everybody stared at us; this large black woman taking a bite out of a little old white woman.

I let go of her, drew myself up to the whole five foot five and a half inches of me, and with all the dignity I could muster, announced, "It's okay, I wasn't really going to eat her. She needs salt." And then I walked away.

XXX ⸻ XX ⸻

Throughout my life, what has kept me going has been my humor and my heritage. Both have fueled my careers as an actress, writer, and, well, unofficial cultural ambassador. And I've always been hungry for more contact and understanding between my African culture and the world at large. Over the years, I have broadened my knowledge of African culture as a whole, and I've found that there's no better way to develop an appreciation of the unique spirit and creativity of an oppressed people than to talk about their food. I started to research African cuisine, and discovered a vast range of recipes—and a lot of public interest—so I decided to write a book.

I wrote that first book, *A Taste of Africa*, in the hope that it would provide a catalyst for conversation between all cultures, and make visible the very real link between black cultures around the globe.

Before the book came out, a good friend and I devised a sort of a portable cooking show that I called "Cuisine Africaine: Tasty Bits and Spicy Tales." The idea was to give African dinner parties in people's homes, and spice the meals with a little theater. The hosts could invite their family and friends and have a great time with no hassles; no concerns about drunk driving or finding a baby-sitter. It was like going out for dinner theater without ever leaving your house; except the hosts got the cook, the storyteller, and performer all in one.

It was an instant hit. This gregarious African girl could now use her cooking skills and her talking and performance abilities to entertain people and enlighten them about her culture. While they ate delicious African food, I regaled them with stories from my life and traditional African tales. I had always dreamed of a career that involved performing, even when I was told nice girls didn't go on stage. My pleasure was only increased when *A Taste of Africa* was made into a television series, and I found myself on African soil shooting segments for my own TV program—a dream come true.

XOX :::::: X X ::::::

Using food as a medium of performance is not a new concept. But as a black woman, using food as performance opens one up to a number of political interpretations and questions. Black women have always had a delicious relationship with food. To this day, for most black women around the world, food still means life, not guilt. Modern society has groomed us to denounce the nurturing aspects of ourselves and this largely includes food and the eating of it. Therein lies the power.

With the tales that follow, scenes from my life and my culture, I invite you to join me in your very own African dinner party. In my African culture, we celebrate many, many rites of passage: the naming of a newborn baby, the purification of a mother after the baby's birth, showing the baby the way to its father's house, the birth of the third boy or girl in a family, puberty rituals, marriage, birthdays, recovery from illness, escaping accidents…the list goes on and on. In telling the stories that follow, I realize that I have crafted a sort of tale of rites of passage in my own life—the things I have lived through, both good and bad, that made me the woman I am today. Myself, I choose to celebrate all of these moments—the joyous and the painful alike—because they are all pieces of who I am, and lessons in how we gain strength. I invite you to celebrate with me.

In Ghana, no celebration is complete without the pouring of a libation—a liquid offering that you pour ceremonially while calling out incantations, prayers, thanks, and invitations to the spirits of long-dead ancestors. One pours a libation privately or at ceremonies, at gatherings, and always prior to any important event.

This practice is still very prevalent in West Africa today. While simple water can be used, these days tradition dictates strong spirits, such as palm wine, schnapps, or gin. Indeed, whenever West Africans open a bottle of spirits, they pour the first few drops on the ground, as an offering to the ancestors, before pouring drinks for anybody else.

Although both serious and inspiring, libation can also be fun. I love to host parties, and will often concoct one of my "lethal weapon" rum cocktails for any of a range of specific invocations. The following concoctions don't necessarily match specific occasions; I like to create drinks that suit my friends' different personalities.

I WAS NEVER HERE…

What follow are my Lethal Weapon 5. The method of producing them is the same in each case, only the ingredients vary. So I've only given instructions for the first. Each produces enough for a party, and should serve about twelve (allowing two drinks per person) or twenty (just one shot for each person). Remember, it's bad luck to drink before the libation is poured.

✖✖ 1. TROPICAL DELIGHT ✖✖

3 cups (24 fl oz/750 ml) white rum
4 cups (32 fl oz/1 liter) mixed tropical fruit juices
     (mango, guava, pineapple, etc.)
1 cup (8 fl oz/250 ml) peach liqueur
Lots of crushed ice

Place all of the liquid ingredients, along with two cups of crushed ice, in a blender or food processor and blend together. Put small amounts of crushed ice in cocktail glasses and pour the drink mix over the ice. Serve immediately, without garnish.

✖✖ 2. MAN-GO-TANGO ✖✖

3 cups (24 fl oz/750 ml) white rum
4 cups (32 fl oz/1 liter) mango juice
1 cup (8 fl oz/250 ml) mango liqueur
Lots of crushed ice

✖✖ 3. ROOTS ✖✖

3 cups (24 fl oz/750 ml) white rum
4 cups (32 fl oz/1 liter) mango juice
1 cup (8 fl oz/250 ml) coconut liqueur
2 teaspoons (10 g) grated gingerroot
Lots of crushed ice

✕✕ 4. PINING FOR YOU ✕✕

3 cups (24 fl oz/750 ml) white rum
4 cups (32 fl oz/I liter) pineapple juice
$^1/_2$ cup (4 fl oz/125 ml) pineapple liqueur
$^1/_2$ cup (4 fl oz/125 ml) coconut liqueur
Lots of crushed ice

✕✕ 5. THE BLACKER THE BERRY ✕✕
THE SWEETER THE JUICE

3 cups (24 fl oz/750 ml) white rum
4 cups (32 fl oz/I liter) black currant juice
I cup (8 fl oz/250 ml) dark plum liqueur
$^1/_2$ cup (4 fl oz/125 ml) raspberry liqueur
$^1/_2$ cup (4 fl oz/125 ml) strawberry liqueur
Lots of crushed ice

If you can't find fresh black currant juice in your local store, you can make it by combining half a cup (4 fl oz/125 ml) Ribena or other black currant syrup with three cups (24 fl oz/750 ml) ice-cold water, and mixing well. You can substitute other berry-flavored liqueurs for the strawberry and raspberry, if you so desire.

✕✕✕ ⸗⸗⸗ ✕ ✕ ⸗⸗⸗

The drink that follows is another festive favorite. It serves two, but you might find it more fun to share one glass with an intimate friend. You can find the silver powder in specialty baking shops; it's often used to ice wedding cakes and other fancy confections.

✖✖ KNIGHTS IN SHINING ARMOR ✖✖

1 tablespoon (15 g) edible silver powder
1 cup (8 fl oz/250 ml) vanilla ice cream
1 1/2 cups (12 fl oz/375 ml) Black Sambucca or Opal
Nero liqueur

Chill two large, long-stemmed glasses in the freezer overnight. Sprinkle two teaspoons of silver powder inside and outside the glasses, making sure you cover them thoroughly, right up to the top. Reserve the third teaspoon for later, and place the glasses carefully back in the freezer.

In a blender or food processor, combine the ice cream and one cup of the liqueur. When thoroughly blended, pour the mixture carefully into the two glasses, filling them about three-quarters of the way. Be careful not to disturb the silver powder any more than necessary. Pour the remaining liqueur over the top, dividing it evenly between the two glasses. Sprinkle with the reserved silver powder and serve with decorative straws. Serve immediately. Cheers!

✖✖✖ ✖ ✖ ✖✖✖

Now I say "Asenta," which means "Guess what happened?" You must answer "Oba," which means "Tell us...we receive you." And now I may begin telling you my story.

My Daddy: A. K. or Naatse or Ayitey Kojo Addy

I WAS NEVER HERE...

The First Time I Ever Cooked for My Father

I haven't always been a respected African cook, but I've known for a long time that food is the quickest way to win friends or make enemies.

I remember the first time I ever cooked for my father. I was about five years old, and I had determined to make him a proper English breakfast. Why a little African girl chose to start her culinary career with one fried egg on toast, covered with black pepper and decorated with tomato slices, I'm not quite sure. I suppose in those days that was the breakfast of choice for Ghana's educated elite and my father, a medical professional, certainly qualified.

My mum and dad had bought me a little oblong tin stove, a miniature version of my mum's cast iron wood-burning cookstove. It was quite an amazing device, really, which ran on the same methylated spirit tablets we used to light our lanterns in those days before we had electricity.

To operate my little stove, I had merely to insert a fuel tablet in the bottom of the oven and light it. The heat from that tablet radiated upwards to hot plates on the top of the stove, making it work (well, more or less, anyway) just like a real range. (I was supervised by my aunty Aduorkor, but it's not uncommon in Africa for children to be entrusted with fire at a much earlier age than their overseas counterparts.) That morning, I took my little saucepan, put it on top of the hot stove, and melted a bit of Blueband margarine in it. I fried up a wild guinea fowl egg, sprinkling it with a little bit of salt as I had seen Mum do. Oops, more salt than I'd intended. No problem, I'd just cover the salt taste with a little bit of Mum's black pepper and some of her white pepper, thrown in for good measure. Two quick sneezes followed, right over the pan, and I forgot to cover my nose—a taboo, but luckily no one saw me. I turned the egg over. And by the time I was finished with that egg, it was more than well-done on both sides. It was, in fact, totally massacred. I hadn't noticed because while it was cooking I used the stove's second hot plate to heat up water in my kettle. I wanted to make my father "Milo tea"—a malt cocoa drink similar to Ovaltine. Then I sliced some tomatoes.

I put the poor crusty egg on one of my little plastic plates, pushed the saucepan to one side, and toasted the bread on top of the hot stove. I could only manage one side of it, because I was worried that the egg was getting cold. Indeed, it was quite cold by the time it got to my father, but there it was: the egg in the middle, a roughly cut triangular half-piece of bread on the side, and a cup of hot Milo. Well, lukewarm Milo anyway. I arranged my masterpiece on a miniature tray and proudly took it in to my unsuspecting father. Setting the tray on the side of the bed, I shook him awake.

"Good morning, Daddy, I've brought your breakfast."

To this day I remember his huge grin and the anticipatory joy on his face; I also remember how that grin froze as he surveyed his breakfast tray. (He was not a man who liked to miss his sleep.) Nonetheless, he sat up in bed and said, "Thank you. Thank you, my darling, for this beautiful breakfast," and he smacked his lips and rubbed his hands together in brave appreciation.

I sat beside him, keenly watching his sleepy face as he swallowed—with difficulty—each oversalted mouthful of what I now realize was a dreadful-looking fried egg. He smiled at me between mouthfuls, and did not speak again until he'd finished.

I was very proud. The moment he'd swallowed the last bite and drained his cup, I ran out of the room to tell my mother how I had cooked Daddy's breakfast and how much he'd loved it. And could I make breakfast for him again tomorrow?

I didn't cook again for my dad for many, many years.

XXXX ===== XX X =====

But, you know, years later I made it up to him. When I was fourteen, Daddy got posted to a country town called Kibi to take charge of the operating theater there. On school holidays, Mum sent me out there to keep him company since she couldn't go herself—she was too busy delivering babies in Kumasi.

To this day, I love spending time with my father. He is mischievous, wise, and a born comic. Whenever I was disobedient, Mum would send me to Dad to be disciplined. Dad would ask me to shut the door and then, putting his arm around my shoulders, he'd say, "I don't know what all this is about but if it upsets your Mum, then try not to do it, okay? Now go, and if Mum should ask, just tell her I've disciplined you." And we'd shake hands to seal our secret.

One afternoon when I was staying with him in Kibi, I decided to cook him chicken stew and rice for dinner. I actually managed it quite well, except that the rice was hard and crunchy. The next time I had a go, the rice was far too mushy, so we agreed that from then on he'd cook the rice and I'd cook the stews. And so we fed each other well for the rest of my holidays.

In the evenings, we would play dominoes, or sometimes he would reenact various traditional stories for me, growling like a leopard and roaring like a lion as he paced about the house. Truly, he was a wonderful storyteller—a gift that he was often able to use for personal advantage. On nights when he wanted to go out with his friends, he'd tell me terrifying ghost stories to frighten me so that I'd go straight to bed and hide underneath the bedclothes until morning. You see, in Western countries parents tell their children fairy tales to lull them into sleep, but in Africa we tell our children spooky stories so they'll be too scared to leave the bed until sunrise. It works quite well.

Here is one of the stories he told me:

𝒳𝒪𝒳 ﹗﹗﹗ 𝒳 𝒳 ﹗﹗﹗   SCARY GHOST STORY   𝒳𝒪𝒳 ﹗﹗﹗ 𝒳 𝒳 ﹗﹗﹗

O nce there were two twin sisters. One was very beautiful and had everything going for her: a good voice and nice hair, in addition to which she was good at sports and clever in school. The other sister, however, was plain-looking, clumsy, slow in school, and had ugly, matted, hard-to-comb hair. In fact, her only talent was that she could speak to birds. The pretty girl was named Atta Panin, elder twin, and the plain one Atta Kakra, younger twin, but everyone called them Panin and Kakra.

The twins' parents loved them both dearly, but spent much of their time worrying about the plain sister, particularly since everybody in their village lavished so much attention on the pretty one. However, being clever people, they never made a fuss about their worries, but tried to treat the two girls equally.

One day, they bought each of the twins the present she wanted most in the world: a jumprope for Panin and a parrot for Kakra. While Panin skipped prettily through the village, Kakra spent her time in the woods, alone with her beloved parrot. She understood his language perfectly, but she wanted him to understand human speech as well. Not sure how her parents would take this, she thought it best to keep the whole project a secret.

I WAS NEVER HERE...

Now, unbeknownst to Kakra, there was another regular visitor to those woods—a handsome young warrior from two villages up the road. His beloved hawk had been injured, and he was teaching it to use its wounded wings again. Kakra didn't know about the warrior, but she often heard the hawk overhead, whining about how much it hurt to fly, and cursing the human who forced him to do this painful thing. She called out kind words to the hawk, never realizing that his master was watching from his hiding place. He was fascinated by this girl—how could she understand what his hawk's cries meant? And how could she answer in kind? He was pretty good with birds, but not as good as her.

After a few days of watching Kakra with the birds, the young warrior decided to make himself known to her. He filled his hands with grain and, when Kakra's parrot flew into the woods ahead of her (as he always did), the young man held out his hands and offered the treats to the bird. Kakra came upon this scene, the two humans got to talking, and soon realized that their love of animals drew them to each other. They made plans to meet again and, before long, word got out that Kakra, the plain twin, was keeping company with a handsome, respected, rich young warrior. In fact, she was going to marry him!

As such talk spread, Panin became increasingly jealous of her younger sister, and hatched a wicked plan to do away with her forever. That way she, not her undeserving, ugly sister would get to marry the warrior. When she learned that the warrior would not be able to meet Kakra in the woods during the next week, as he was supervising preparations for their wedding, she knew she had to act.

For days, Panin worked in secret, stringing together many colorful seeds to make a beautiful bead necklace. When it was finished, she knew it was irresistible. She got up early one morning to put her evil plan in action. Venturing into the woods, she went straight to a big pond that lay in the middle of the trees, and swam out in the deepest water. Now remember, Panin was not just beautiful but athletic, and a very good swimmer. Poor Kakra couldn't swim at all. Wicked Panin sprinkled handfuls of delicious grains over the big green water lily leaves that floated over that deep water, and placed the beautiful bead necklace on the water lily that lay over the very deepest spot of all. That finished, she went home to bed, knowing that Kakra's parrot wouldn't be able to resist those tasty grains on the water lilies—the water lilies floating over the very deepest water.

Sure enough, the trick worked. As Kakra's parrot soared ahead of her into the woods, like he always did, he spotted the grains laid out on the lilies and squawked with delight. Who could have been so thoughtful, he asked. Oh, it must be the love-stricken warrior. But wait, what's that colorful thing glinting amidst the grains? He flew closer to inspect, and saw the seed necklace. For his bride to be, what a romantic, he called out to Kakra, and they both danced with joy. The bird swooped down to eat the grain, and Kakra followed to see the beautiful necklace he'd described. She had often played in the shallow end of this pond and, not being a swimmer, had no idea how quickly it could get deep. Suddenly, the ground fell out from under her and she sank straight down. Way out of her depth, she thrashed around, struggling for air and trying desperately to grab onto something, but there was nothing there. She couldn't even reach the beautiful lilies.

Her parrot realized that his mistress was in mortal danger, and tried to dive in and pull her out by the hair, but he just wasn't strong enough. (At this point, Dad would pretend to be a bird—clasping his fingers in the shape of a beak, he'd try and "peck" the cover off my bed.) In panic, the poor bird flew as fast as he could to Kakra's house to sound an alarm. (Here, Dad would flap his arms and "fly" around my bedroom squawking like a bird.) Her family rushed to follow him, but they arrived too late. Kakra had drowned in the pond.

Her parents were distraught and the warrior inconsolable. Her parrot just sat on a perch outside her bedroom all day, rocking back and forth and calling out her name: Kakra, Kakra, Kakra. Panin, stricken too late with the enormity of what she'd done, was too guilt-ridden to admit it. Indeed, she went mute and never spoke another word the rest of her life.

But legend has it that the ghost of poor plain Kakra still calls out from ponds around the country, in an attempt to warn off other innocent young girls from the waters.

Here, Dad would drop his voice and almost whisper: "She has even been seen at night by the pond down the road from our house.

"Sometimes she arrives in the dead of night like a breeze through the bedroom windows to warn young girls in their sleep to watch where they tread. Other times, when girls walk alone, the ghost appears behind them as the shadow, to warn them never to trust anyone, not even their own shadow."

Suddenly, Dad would stop and look nervously around the room, whistling and making eerie wind noises. "Can you hear that wind rustling through the trees outside? Perhaps it's Kakra's ghost, come to pay you a visit. I'd better leave you girls to your private talks!" And with that, he'd tiptoe out of my bedroom, leaving me alone.

After a story like that, I'd be so scared that I would pull the covers over my head and lie absolutely still, no matter how sweltering the night, until I eventually dropped off to sleep.

⁕⧫⁕ ⁙⁙⁙ ✕ ✕ ⁙⁙⁙

Dad always built his stories to a slow crescendo, using action, sounds, and dramatic pauses to increase the tension to a mesmerizing (and sometimes paralyzing!) finale. Although I knew all of this, he was so good at storytelling and playacting that I almost always got sucked in. Not every story was frightening, however. Sometimes he used his skills to teach another kind of lesson, as on one morning in Kibi when he woke up with a terrible cough. I wanted him to stay home so I could take care of him, but Daddy insisted on going to work. I got very upset with him, as I couldn't understand why he wouldn't give himself a little rest so he could get better. Daddy just said that his patients needed him, but to calm me down, he told me a story before he left for the day:

XOX ⠿ X X ⠿

One day a messenger in the form of a bird came to the animals' village and announced that Elephant had lost his mother. Everybody was very sad and, being true friends and true village folk, they always helped each other. So they decided that they would help Elephant bury his mother. Elephant's mother had lived at least five villages away; it was a whole day's journey to get there, and everybody had to bring a little present or something to eat.

Well, Tortoise thought about this. He thought, Hang on a minute, I walk very slowly. Everybody will go and they will get there at the end of the day, but I probably won't get there until the end of the week, after they have buried Elephant's mother and already come back. So he planned his trip very carefully.

He called out to Donkey, "Hei, Brother Donkey, you're my good friend. Can you help me?"

Donkey said, "Of course, Brother Tortoise, that's what friends are for."

"I've not been feeling too well lately," said Tortoise. "I won't be able to attend Elephant's mother's funeral, but I still want to send my gift with you; just a little parcel to help with funeral costs and feeding the masses who will come for the wake. I know that everybody is going to leave before sunrise, so early tomorrow morning, would you come by my place? I will leave a little parcel on the front doorstep. If you could take it with you and deliver it for me as my contribution, I would be very grateful."

Donkey said, "No problem. But you go to bed now, Brother Tortoise, you don't look too well. Go and have a rest."

Sure enough, early next morning, Donkey came past Tortoise's house, dutifully picked up the parcel, and carefully carried it all the way along the plains, through the tall grass and through the forest, over mountains, across valleys and rivers, until he got to Elephant's mother's funeral.

Everybody sat in a circle and deposited their presents in the middle. When it came to be Donkey's turn, he deposited his present, saying, "Oh, by the way, Tortoise couldn't come because he wasn't very well. But he asked me to deliver his present for him and here it is."

Donkey set Tortoise's present down in the center of the circle and when he unraveled it, guess what? Tortoise came tumbling out of the parcel. He had found a clever way for Donkey to carry him. In spite of the fact that they were at a funeral, everybody burst out laughing and congratulated Tortoise on his cleverness.

"And the moral of the story is," my daddy said, looking hard at me to make sure I was listening, "whenever your body lets you down, you've got to let your mind work for you. Don't ever forget that. Your mind is always in charge of your body."

XOX ═════ X X ═════

Now that I'm older, I think about that story when my mind tells me, for instance, that I can disco-dance until the small hours of the morning, and still plan to work a full day afterwards, or that I can play soccer as nimbly as my young ones. All too often, though, my body tells me otherwise.

So it was a good story, Daddy, but the moral's not entirely true. My mind is happy to be in charge, but my body's not too interested in listening. It seems it's got a bit of an attitude problem and a mind of its own.

Here are some of the recipes my father and I cooked in Kibi.

✕✕ NAA TSENKUA'S FLOR ✕✕

*(Translation: "flor" is "stew" in the Ga dialect, and
Naa Tsenkua is my Ghanaian name.)*

SERVES 2

2 cups (1 lb/$^1/_2$ kg) diced lean beef or lamb

Salt

Ground black pepper

3–4 tablespoons (3–4 oz/30–40 g) cornstarch

1/2 cup (4 fl. oz/125 ml) vegetable oil

2 large onions, peeled and diced

1 red Thai chile pepper with seeds, finely chopped

1 green bell pepper, seeded and finely chopped

2 teaspoons (10 g) finely grated fresh ginger

4 medium tomatoes, blanched in boiling water,
    peeled, and diced

4 cups (32 fl. oz/1 liter) water

$^1/_2$ ounce (15 g) thick tomato paste

8 ounces (250 g) small button mushrooms

Season the meat to taste with salt and pepper. Dredge the meat in the cornstarch, making sure that it is well coated.

Heat the vegetable oil in a heavy skillet and fry the meat until lightly browned. Remove it from the oil and set aside.

Fry the onions, chile, bell pepper, and ginger in the remaining oil until the onions turn translucent.

Add the tomatoes, meat, water, tomato paste, and mushrooms. Stir well and season to taste with salt and pepper. Lower the heat, and allow the stew to simmer slowly until the meat is soft and the sauce somewhat reduced and thickened.

Serve hot with steamed long-grain rice and a salad of Swiss chard or spinach.

I WAS NEVER HERE...

✖✖ DADDY'S PICK-ME-UP CHILE AND RICE ✖✖ BREAKFAST DISH

SERVES 2

$1/_2$ cup (4 fl oz/125 ml) red palm oil
I onion, peeled and chopped very fine
I red Thai chile pepper
I large tomato, finely chopped
I tablespoon (15 g) grated fresh ginger
I tablespoon (15 g) dried shrimp powder,
  or ground dry shrimp
I tablespoon (15 g) finely chopped fresh
  green shrimp or prawns
I cup (8 oz/250 g) cooked black-eyed peas
Steamed rice
2 whole lettuce leaves
Optional garnish: parsley, basil, sliced
  hard-boiled eggs

Melt the red palm oil in a heavy skillet, then fry the onions in it until they are just browned. Add the chile pepper, tomato, and ginger, and cook for another two minutes.

Add the powdered or ground shrimp, fresh shrimp or prawns, and black-eyed peas, and stir well. Taste, and adjust seasoning with salt and pepper if necessary.

Cook on low heat, stirring constantly, for three to five minutes. Thoroughly mix with some steamed long-grain rice and serve hot, scooped out into individual rounds on lettuce leaves. Garnish with parsley, basil, or sliced hard-boiled eggs if you wish.

✕✕ EGG DISH ✕✕

*A similar recipe is thought to have been brought to Jamaica by
dispossessed slaves. Over time, it evolved into ackee and saltfish, which
many regard as the Jamaican national dish.*

SERVES 2

I medium dry-salted codfish or tilapia

$^1/_2$ ounce (15g) butter

2 tablespoons (I fl oz/30 ml) corn or olive oil

2 cloves garlic, peeled and finely chopped

I large onion, peeled and finely chopped

I medium green bell pepper, seeded and
   finely chopped

4 fresh free-range guinea fowl eggs
   (ordinary large eggs can be substituted)

Freshly ground white pepper

2–3 leaves spinach or Swiss chard, cleaned,
   destalked, and finely sliced into ribbons

Soak the fish in lots of cold water overnight to soften it and to
remove the salt. In the morning, rinse the fish several times in cold water
to remove as much salt as possible (taste a small piece to be sure). Shred
the fish into small slivers, checking for and removing any bones. Set aside.
Should yield about one cup (8 oz/250 g) of fish.

Melt the butter and oil in a deep frying pan on medium heat. Fry
the fish, garlic, onion, and bell pepper together for about 7–10 minutes,
stirring constantly.

Push the fish mixture to the sides, making a well in the middle of the
pan. Crack the eggs into the center of this well. Add a pinch of white pepper, turn up the heat to medium high, and scramble the eggs very quickly.
When they're cooked, mix the scrambled eggs into the fish mixture and
add the ribbons of spinach or chard. Stir lightly to mix the lot, then turn
the heat down very low. Cook for one more minute and serve hot with
boiled vegetables, such as yams, taro, plantains, green bananas, or cassava.

I WAS NEVER HERE...

My Mother's Wisdom

My mother was a complex woman—at once my staunchest defender and my fiercest adversary. In many ways, I can say that I am what I am today because of her; she pushed me hard to achieve her standards of perfection, much as I push myself today. I like to think that I have more fun in the process, however.

Mother's family belonged to the Accra establishment. Her father's brother, Charles Woolhouse Bannerman, had been the first black judge elected in Ghana during the colonial days, and her father, Sam Bannerman (my grandpa), worked as a supreme court registrar. These brothers and their families were high-society ladies and gentlemen, schooled in the proper British eloquence and manners so valued at the time.

Since childhood, my mother has been addressed by everyone around her as Awula Naa Lamiley Bannerman, meaning Lady Naa Lamiley Bannerman. My aunt Betty, her younger sister, is still called Awuraba, meaning younger lady. Indeed, as it is considered disrespectful for Ghanaian children to address adults by their first names, we always called my aunt Betty Aunty Awuraba—literally, "Aunty Lady."

My mother, coming from such a high-status background, worried about my turning out right. To this end, I received many beatings as a child, some quite severe; and all of them, according to my mother, did indelible good to my soul. Sometimes she even gave me prophylactic beatings, just in case I was thinking of being naughty. I have, as an adult, discovered that this practice was not unique to my mother—many of my friends' mothers seem to have done the same!

Still, my mother was a stickler for justice, and a fearless champion of women and children. In addition to running a maternity hospital with my aunty Thelma, she was forever taking care of other peoples' children, often letting them stay in our house. It seemed like she followed the progress of every child she'd delivered and if, years later, it seemed they weren't thriving, she'd invite the youngster over regularly for hot Milo and powdered milk drinks to insure they got proper nourishment.

And it didn't end there. Whenever she had traditional clothes made up at the dressmaker's, she would insist that any leftover fabric be transformed into child-sized garments, which she gave away to her little charges when they came over to be fed.

She was always fighting the good fight, whether against outsiders, such as the foreign drug companies trying to dump drugs into our community for testing, or against her own neighbors. One of the most heartbreaking of those latter fights was with husbands and older women from certain tribal groups who wanted their wives and baby girls circumcised.

A lot of the older women had been circumcised themselves, which usually meant a radical clitoridectomy, leaving just the labia majora. The practice was common enough that many, many people still believed that this was the right and proper way for a woman to be in order to satisfy her man. So, the elder women were often the most ardent proponent of this horrible practice, and the men would enlist their support in petitioning my mother.

*My Mummy: Awura
Elizabeth Naa Lamiley
Bannerman-Addy*

"Excuse me Madame," they would say, "but our culture says that we must respect the word of the older woman, and my aunty here is older than you. Oh, I know you are an educated midwife and have no doubt learnt plenty from books, but she is a custodian of our traditional ways, and you should respect her word."

That always flummoxed my mother because she knew, theoretically, that they were right. But that didn't stop her. She'd try saying things like, "But the baby will get blood poisoning," explaining what a horrible fate that would be.

Sometimes that worked, but all too often, the aunty would reply, "Well, I didn't get blood poisoning. Here I am, alive."

In those cases, Mum would have to quickly recall the family's medical history, and remind them of how many of their baby girls *had* died. Even if the girls hadn't been circumcised, she would say, "But you see, those baby girls who died were *afraid* to suffer the mutilation. That's why their spirits left you."

Now of course if there had been no such deaths in the family, she'd have to find a different story. Usually, she would tell them that the baby in question was not well and that nothing could be done at least for a while, until it was out of harm's way.

Still, she could only do so much against the force of tradition. One of the very few times I ever saw my mother cry was after a little girl whom she had once protected came to her at the age of thirteen to show Mum what had been done to her. Mum was devastated. She turned to me and said, "My God, I try so hard to protect them, but once they are grown, I have no control. How many more are out there, Naa Tsenkua? How many more have I missed?"

I didn't know what to say. I still don't.

XX XX X X XX

Even though I often felt abandoned or hard-pressed by my mother, I realize now that she was a woman of amazing strength and wisdom. Indeed, I sometimes hear myself quoting from her vast repertoire of spot-on sayings:

When an adult man behaves poorly:
> He did what? And him a grown man with pubic hairs and hairy gums. He ought to know better.

When I complain that the kids are running around like crazy after dinner:
> Oh, leave them alone Dorinda. Belly dey full, monkey dey jump.

When I complain about others insulting me:
> Insults never left lumps on the body, so who cares?

When I'm so stressed out about a deadline that I won't sleep:
That's ridiculous. Just because you die doesn't mean
you can't go to sleep.

Anytime someone commended my siblings or myself on our behavior:
Oh yes, angel abroad, devil at home.

If anyone forgets to return a favor:
Hand go, hand come.

When I told her I was thinking of marrying again:
What do you need to get married for? All you need is
a man to periodically paint your clouds.

For someone who can't keep confidences:
They have not learnt that inside every head there is a lounge
and a bedroom. The private matters should stay in the bedroom
undisturbed. Lounge matters are for public consumption.

When I complained about my siblings being awful:
Even though your gums may be rotten, you've no choice but
to keep licking them!

When someone gets boastful and bigheaded:
A big head doesn't necessarily carry the wisdom of the world.

When someone is selfish with food:
Let them eat it. It's only glorified waste, it will come out
sooner or later.

Finally, some wise words from my grandmother:
In this world, to be too stupid serves little purpose and to be
too wise attracts resentment, but a little stupidity mixed with a
healthy dose of wisdom moves mountains and still leaves you
human.

Shooshoonsha, Shoonsha

The chapter title refers to the noises my family would make, rhythmically, to encourage me to perform. But far more often, it seemed to me, they wanted to encourage me to do more mundane tasks. Beginning when I was very young, my mother entrusted me with responsibilities far beyond my years. I suppose that was her way of complimenting me, really, because it was like saying, "I know you are capable and reliable and you will execute any task I give you efficiently." Being a resourceful girl, there were many times when I exploited these opportunities, and this is a story about one of them that turned out extraordinarily well for me.

I can't remember exactly how old I was when the following events took place. I think I would have been somewhere around three or four, but my mother argues that it was closer to five. Anyway, it happened around the time that my mother and my Aunt Thelma introduced the revolutionary concept of prenatal care to the women in our area, in an attempt to reduce infant and maternal mortality through proper nutrition and regular checkups. This approach proved to be so successful that before long they found it necessary to set up regular prenatal classes and clinics every Tuesday and Thursday; my job was to keep an eye on the children of the pregnant mothers who had come to attend these clinics.

I got to look after anywhere from three to six children at a time. Because I was a child myself, I couldn't really baby-sit them per se, but I could certainly entertain them and keep them out of everybody's hair. (Aunty Jane, a hired nursing assistant, was there to help with any children wanting to be taken to the toilet or needing their diapers changed.)

After a time, the success of Thelma's prenatal clinics reached the ears of the Asantehene Otomfuo Nana Agyeman Prempeh, the Ashanti Royal Chief. As was customary, His Royal Highness had many wives, and he recommended that all of them attend the clinics. (I often wondered how many wives he had, but it would have been impolite to ask, so I never did.) Thus, Mum and Aunt Thelma became the midwives-elect to the royal family, a very great honor. Out of respect for the monarchy, Aunt Thelma and Mum arranged to start the clinic for the royal wives two hours earlier than the rest of the patients. They'd begin looking after the royal wives at six o'clock in the morning and usually be finished by half past seven; that gave them half an hour's break to have a cup of tea or coffee, write their reports, and tidy up before everybody else came for the regular clinic.

The official starting time for my child-care assignment was a quarter past eight, but I was eager to see (and entertain) the royal children. Without going into why, I convinced my mother to bring me in with her to the early clinic. But to my surprise, the royal wives did not bring any of their children along—they didn't have to. The children were all being looked after by their grannies and their extended families. But I was all fired up to entertain *someone*, so I wasn't going to let the lack of children, my usual audience, stop me. I was going to perform!

Indeed, I have always loved to perform. As far back as I can remember, I entertained myself and others by singing and dancing.

As a child, one of my favorite places to do this was in front of the radio, especially the Big Bandstand Hour, which just happened to air right around 6 AM, and featured such greats as the Glen Miller Band. Ah, the happy hours I spent with Glen Miller. I loved the music; it was hot, fast, and exciting and I never missed an opportunity to listen. Indeed, I never missed a beat. Sometimes I would make up my own dance steps, other times I would copy the moves I had seen the older children doing, and add embellishments of my own. It occurred to me that adults would be impressed by my prowess and so, when the royal wives showed up for their appointments, I was ready.

I waited until my mother and Aunt Thelma went inside the examination room with their first patient, and then I ran to the little room just off the reception area, switched on the radio, and began my routine. I danced into the waiting room with one hand on my hip, the other waving wildly in the air in my best rendition of the jitterbug. A twirl or two and I switched over to twisting my hips one way, bending my knees, gyrating—anything went. The women loved it, they clapped and laughed hysterically. Every time I heard the squeak of the examination room door, I'd switch off the radio and run to sit quietly before my mother came in to call for the next patient. This made the women laugh even more. Mum thought I was amusing them with the clever recitations she'd taught me, and the royal women were loyal. They knew exactly what I was up to, and they never once told my mum.

I'm sure those women were more than a bit nervous about coming to be examined. Accustomed to being treated with a certain measure of respect, they didn't know what to expect in this new situation. And while my mother was always respectful, that didn't excuse them from being interviewed, having their fingers pricked for a blood test, being asked to pass urine into a test tube, and being weighed, prodded, and squeezed in various intrusive ways. My little show must

I WAS NEVER HERE...

have brought a kind of light relief for them. And, of course, I was delighted; I had a captive audience because the poor things couldn't go anywhere else except to the toilet. It became a regularly scheduled performance for the royal wives.

At the finish, when the last patient had gone in, I would, for my pièce de résistance, bring out a battered old saucepan and pass it around so my audience could show their appreciation with donations of sweets, money, or other gifts. Sometimes I'd make as much as two pounds in cash ($3.50). On those rare occasions, I'd bring out my two spoons and play them over my knee for an encore. I was a real ham.

Sooner or later, my mother had to find out what was really going on. And she did, sooner rather than later. Let's just say she was not impressed, but she controlled her anger whilst the patients were there.

"How could you embarrass me like that?" she demanded when the last patient had left. "You've been taking presents from strangers, collecting money from paying patients. Can't you see it's like double dipping? People will think we're desperate. And as for that cheap dance, it's unladylike and vulgar."

No, I couldn't see her point. I was crushed. The gifts were for me, for a job well done. How could she say those things? My dances made people laugh, they were fun, people loved them.

But my opinion didn't matter. I never danced at Thelma's Maternity Home again. From then on, Mum got some toys and made me sit and play with the children in another room, cut off from the pre-natal patients. Still, something wondrous did come of my unladylike gyrations.

One Tuesday after the early clinic, I heard one of the royal wives ask Mum, "Can we see your little girl? We want her to come and entertain us."

My mother replied, "Well, she's got things to do..."

But the woman insisted. Apparently, the previous week Mum had promised them they could see me, and she knew that if she didn't produce me soon, they'd still be sitting there when the next batch of patients arrived. So I was hauled out in front of the royal wives. This time I did not dance. For some reason, I actually felt quite shy, as though I'd never seen them before. I dropped my head down and stared at my feet.

The women started to run their hands through my hair and along my scalp and forehead. "She is one of us," they declared. "Look at her broad forehead. She is an Ashanti Royal. Feel." And they passed me from woman to woman for examination.

After a while I began to think that maybe they were using this as an opportunity to pay back my mother for all those months of prodding them in her examination room.

One of the royal wives, Nana Akua, said to my mother, "Let me take this child back with me to the palace. Don't let her waste her gifts dancing to the radio; I will take responsibility for teaching her how to do the Adowa dances, the traditional dances of the Ashanti people, and we will also teach her our songs."

And right there in the waiting room of Thelma's Maternity Home, Nana Akua and the Royal wives began to sing. I learned two traditional songs that day, while my mother stood by watching. I think she was a little bit proud, even if she wouldn't admit it.

Before she left that morning, Nana Akua took both my hands in hers and pulled me close to her. Looking into my eyes, she said, "You have a natural talent. There is a spirit to perform inside of you. This gift needs to be encouraged and harnessed, and I will help you." In Ghana, we don't actually have a word for talent, but what she did say meant, "You have the God-given spirit inside of you that gives you the courage to be able to stand up in front of people and show off without shame."

At the time I didn't realize the magnitude of what she was telling me. I just thought that here was a lady who understood how a little girl could enjoy a bit of Glen Miller and make a lot of money. I would have been happy to follow her to the end of the rainbow. Little did any of us know how profound her statement would turn out to be.

An agreement was reached with my mother that each week when Nana Akua came for her prenatal care, she would take me back with her to the palace; she promised she would have me home by lunch time. And that was the beginning of my introduction to the royal household and the traditional court dances, music, drumming, and other fruits of my pure heritage.

It's a shame that Nana Akua, or Aunty Elizabeth as I later came to call her, is no longer around to see what has been borne from the gems of wisdom she planted. Had I followed my early dreams and inclinations, I could well have christened myself Glenda Miller and had my own rock and roll band. Who knows? But I wouldn't have stayed so connected to my African culture, and that connection has yielded so many rewards.

✕◈✕ ⠿⠿ ✕ ✕ ⠿⠿

One hot summer day in my adopted home of Australia, I was relaxing on the grass in a public park, reading. Somewhere in the distance, I became vaguely aware of a child singing. I looked up from my book for a moment and listened, really listened. It was an Akan song from Ghana, a fisherman's song, and it was accompanied by the sound of some rather crude drumming. I slowly cocked my head to the side to see where the sound was coming from. Just a little way off, I saw a mother and father picnicking with two children. The little girl was dancing around and singing, "Sisiribom, tabonobom, sisiribom, tabonobom," a Fanti fisherman's rhythm that I've taught a number of kids over the years, through my program of bringing African culture into the schools. The little boy was drumming on some books with his shoes.

The father said to the children, "What is this rubbish? Where did you get this from?"

Quite calmly, the little girl stopped dancing. She screwed up her nose and looked at her parents, saying, "It's not rubbish, it's an African song. Dorinda showed us at our school. It's very nice, want to learn it?"

"No thank you," the parents replied.

Undaunted, the little girl said, "Watch, I'll show you," and the children carried on with the song. When she had finished, she stood and stared at them, obviously waiting for applause.

The parents clapped half-heartedly, obviously playing along for the sake of the kids.

"Aren't you going to clap properly?" the little girl asked. "You should clap, because that's what you do when you are in an African village. You clap loudly and tell us how wonderful it is. Dorinda said so."

I was stunned, and a little hesitant to reveal my identity at that moment. I waited until the family was about to leave and then I got

up and walked across the grass. As I approached, the little girl recognized me and came running over.

"Dorinda! Dorinda!" She hugged me and, taking me by the hand, led me to her parents. "Mum and Dad, this is Dorinda. She must have heard my song, so she came."

The little boy looked up at me and said, "Hi, Dorinda, I know how to drum now, so can I come to Africa?"

I hugged the kids and thanked the parents for the opportunity to share my culture with their children. For a long time after they left, I stayed glued to the spot with a smile on my face. Out of the thirty-odd thousand children I work with each year, if only one child could carry the song of joy and pass it on, I'm winning.

XXX ⠿⠿ XX ⠿⠿

People always want to know about my visits to the palace—what was it like, what did we eat, what secrets did I learn? Well, this is very difficult for me, because the storyteller in me wants to oblige them, but the Ghanaian cannot. It was a very special privilege to be allowed into the inner sanctum of the Ashanti palace, especially at such a young age, and to divulge the sort of rituals I was allowed to witness there would be the height of ingratitude, truly a betrayal of an almost sacred trust.

I *can* say that I was always awestruck during my times at the palace because I knew that every step I took among those trees on the red, uneven, untarred grounds was almost literally in the footprints of my people's greatest leaders. It was an air of mystery, of ancient history, steeped in secret rituals, libations, and ceremonies the thought of which left me in a constant state of wonder.

And people are curious about the food, to which I answer that the notion of special elegant meals eaten by royalty is a very Western one. The Ashanti royals eat much the same food as everyone else, although the following recipes were particular favorites at the palace:

✕✕ PALMNUT SOUP WITH FUFU ✕✕

SERVES 4–6

$^1/_2$ cup (4 fl oz/125 ml) water

2 pounds (1 kg) lean lamb or beef, cut into chunks

4-6 small segments of salted pigs' trotters, jointed
   and cleaned

Salt and pepper to taste

2 large onions, finely chopped

3 large ripe tomatoes, blanched, peeled, and puréed,
   or 14 fl oz/380ml of canned tomato puree

1 cup (8 fl oz/250 ml) boiling water

28 fl oz/800 g palmnut pulp (available at
   African, West Indian, and Southeast Asian
   specialty stores)

4 large mushrooms, cleaned and peeled

2 giant crabs cooked whole in salted water and
   drained (remove the legs to add separately, but
   leave the claws on)

Chile powder or fresh-ground red chiles, to taste
   (optional)

2 pounds (1 kg) cooked or cured fish fillets (can be
   salted, smoked, grilled, deep-fried, or sun-dried)

Place the water, meat, and pigs' trotters in a 10-quart stock pot and season to taste with salt and pepper. Stir in the chopped onions and cook on medium heat, stirring constantly, until the meat is seared (lightly braised). Add the tomatoes and simmer for 10–15 minutes.

In a large bowl, add the boiling water to the palmnut pulp, beating with a wooden spoon, until the mixture is smooth and creamy. Add this to the simmering pot along with the mushrooms, crabs, and crab legs. Season to taste with chile powder, if desired. Simmer on medium heat for

30–40 minutes, stirring occasionally to prevent ingredients from sticking to the bottom of the pan.

Add your choice of fish either whole or in chunks (be sure to remove any remaining bones) and simmer slowly until soup thickens and the meat is softened. This shouldn't be more than an hour—any longer, and the fish will break up too much and become mushy.

Serve hot with Fufu.

✕✕ FUFU ✕✕

SERVES 4-6

6 cups (48 fl oz/1.5 L) boiling water
5 oz (150 g) potato flour or potato starch
1 1/2 cups (12 fl oz/375 ml) lukewarm water
6 oz (180 g) instant mashed potato flakes

Pour half of the boiling water into a medium-sized saucepan, to warm it.

In a medium-sized mixing bowl blend the potato flour or starch with the lukewarm water, stirring until you have a creamy mixture. The water can't be too hot or it will prematurely cook the starch.

When you are ready to cook, discard the water from the warmed saucepan. Pour the potato flakes into the warm saucepan and add the remaining hot water to cover the flakes. Do not stir yet!

Using a wooden spoon, make sure the potato-flour mixture in the bowl is still runny. If not, stir it and quickly add it to the soaking potato flakes. Speed will be of the essence here! Stir the two mixtures together vigorously, gripping the pan firmly with one hand as you fold the dough from the center against the sides of the pan to mix thoroughly.

When the dough is firm and smooth, wet your hands and form the dough into smooth, medium sized balls. Place them in a small bowl, moistened with cold water to keep the dough from sticking to the surface.

✕✕ KONTOMIRE NE MOMONE ✕✕
(SPINACH WITH SMELLY SALTED FISH)

SERVES 2-4

1 medium dried salted fish (about 8 oz/250g)

2-4 whole baby plantains, peeled

8 slices each taro and yam (about 3 small taro roots
   or 2 small yams)

or 8 small potatoes peeled and diced

2 pounds (1 kg) fresh spinach or Swiss chard,
   washed, stemmed, and chopped

2 small onions, finely chipped

4 small tomatoes, finely diced

4 tablespoons (60 ml) vegetable oil

2 cloves garlic, finely chopped

1 tablespoon (15 g) turmeric

Soak the fish overnight to remove most of the salt. In the morning, rinse, clean, and bone it, then shred it into small pieces and put it aside.

Boil the diced plantains, taro, and yams (or potatoes) in salted water until tender, then drain and set aside. While they're cooking, place the spinach or chard in a colander or vegetable steamer and steam it over the boiling vegetables for about 5–7 minutes.

In a blender or food processor, combine the spinach or chard, onions, tomatoes, and half of the fish pieces until it becomes a smooth paste.

Heat the oil in a small frying pan, then add the garlic and cook until lightly browned. Remove the pan from the heat and stir in the turmeric.

Serve the blended greens mixture in individual bowls. Top each serving with two teaspoons of the turmeric/garlic mixture, then sprinkle with the leftover fish. Decorate each bowl with the boiled root vegetable right before serving. This is a traditional and very nutritious breakfast.

These are the songs that the Ashanti royal women sang for me:

Bonsuo nana eee
Hear me Bonsuo's grandchild

Bonsuo nana nagyemedo ee
Hear me Bonsuo's grandchild who answers me when I call

Kegyatia na wayembonee papa
Kejetia has greatly offended me

Mehuu Naa 'Sei muhuuyanka mamba oo
Had I known Naa 'Sei, I would not have come

Mehuuyanka mamba oo no ee, Eno eniwaa ee
Had I known, I would not have come, dear ancestral mother Eniwa

Kwasea nagyemedo no ee
The idiot has made a fool out of me (in the marketplace)

Mifri Mampong dwa ooo
I'm coming from Mampong market, ooo

Mifri Mampong dwa eee bunuwa ee bunuwa ee
I'm coming from Mampong market, bunuwa ee bunuwa ee

Obi mbehwe nia mede aba ooo
Someone come and see what I have brought, ooo

Obi mfere Nana 'Sei mmame, Obi mfere Nan 'Sei mmame
Someone call Nana 'Sei for me, Someone call Nana 'Sei for me

Nana Osei Agyeman Nana onnie, Agyeman Nana daadaa no eee
Nana Osei Agyeman, here he is, Agyeman Nana now flatter him, eee

Hey, boniama oo, Emaa beku mmarima agya eee
Hey, Booni Ama, ooo. Women will kill the men and leave them eee

In this second song, the implication is not that the women will literally kill the men, but that from time immemorial, women have flattered men to death. Naa 'Sei (or Nana Osei) is clearly someone very important, probably one of our early chiefs.

Songs such as these tend to be about public figures—ruling monarchs or legendary men of valor. They are usually sung by the women on special occasions on which it is appropriate to extol the subject's virtues, although they may also be satirized to recount funny stories about the subject's misdemeanors. They sound rather like the early Caribbean calypso songs and, indeed, it is not unreasonable to assume that the art originated in Ghana and spread with the slave trade to the Islands.

As you can tell above, many of these songs unfortunately lose much of their charm and color when translated into English.

Bamboo Fish

Some of my earliest childhood memories are of my visits to Accra, the capital of Ghana. My parents had grown up in Accra, and much of my family still lived there. So, every August from the time I was three, my parents would send me to stay with those relatives during the holidays while they remained home in Kumasi, 198 miles inland. These visits to the bustling coastal city were interludes of a rare and precious freedom for me, since my mother felt that my status as a member of the educated elite (even at the age of three!) meant that certain types of child's play were forbidden me at home.

Particularly, I was not ever supposed to get dirty. But I just wanted to have some fun, and in Accra I could run wild in the streets with my cousins and their friends, whose parents were less strict. One of our favorite games involved racing homemade bamboo toys, shaped like cuttlefish, in the large open gutters that ran along each side of the roads. We designed and built the toys with speed in mind, painted on elaborate decorations carefully chosen to impress the opposition, and carefully waxed them to prevent the bamboo from getting waterlogged.

These races often took us for miles through town. As the rushing gutter water carried our cuttlefish along, we'd run like hell to keep pace, shouting encouragements to our craft and making rude noises at the kids on opposing teams. At each crossroad the gutter went underground, so we'd rush ahead to wait for our fish's reappearance on the opposite side. And then we were off again, laughing and cheering our racers on, and using sticks (the rule was that you weren't allowed to touch the fish with your hands) to help them maneuver around any floating debris.

The best part, though, was that we collected friends along the way. You might start out with just two kids, gain six as you raced through the next district, and finish up with as many as twenty on each side.

Anywhere along the course, disaster might strike. While the fish rarely sank, they would, every so often, fail to emerge from under a crossroad. Or, more humiliating, a team's fish might become irretrievably lodged in a mass of human waste, in which case the losers would reluctantly concede defeat. No matter what, though, we'd end up hooting and shouting with laughter by race's end—until suddenly we realized, as always, that we were miles from home and had better get back by dark...or else.

So we'd bid our bamboo fish good-bye (because after seeing where they'd been, nobody wanted to touch them), and race home excitedly discussing the next day's race, and our plans for design improvements. Arm in arm, we'd wind our way through the city streets, singing the Fish Song at the top of our lungs.

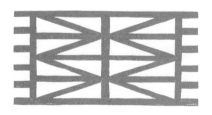

I WAS NEVER HERE...

THE FISH SONG

Koomi kè Loo, Koomi kè Loo, Koomi kè Loo
Kenkey and Fish, Kenkey and Fish, Kenkey and Fish

Ni ame tee amaafo abotri
Went in for a bit of wrestling

Ni ame tee amaafo abotri
Went in for a bit of wrestling

Loo si komisi, Loo si komisi
Fish stamped his feet, Fish stamped his feet

Ni mantsè ǧonti teshi
But Master Big Thumb got up

Ni mantsè ǧonti teshi
But Master Big Thumb got up

Ni eko loo ekèngme komino
And placed Fish 'pon the Kenkey

Ni eko loo ekèngme komino
And placed Fish 'pon the Kenkey

Note: Kenkey is a plain fermented ball of maize dough that is wrapped in corn husks or banana leaves and steamed, like a tamale. It is a cheap and popular staple of the traditional Ghanaian diet, and is usually served topped with fried fish (hence the song), chopped tomatoes and onions, and a variety of pepper sauces.

Ashanti Women

The Western world did not invent the concept of the "super-mom." For years I have marvelled at the grace with which just about any of my countrywomen can breast-feed an infant, hand-feed a toddler, keep an eye on the cooking pot, and run the small provisions store arranged behind them—all at the same time.

On days when the phones are ringing relentlessly, the fax is spewing paper, the milk is boiling over, and the doorbell chimes, all whilst I'm desperately trying to write a gem or two to meet my latest deadline, the thought of my African counterparts cools my heart and gives me the resilience to survive.

Ashanti women are supremely confident. They are astute, vociferous, and hardworking. Nowhere will you find more fiercely devoted mothers, and in business they are adventurous entrepreneurs, the power brokers behind the men. I used to sit in the window of Thelma's Maternity Home and watch the women passing by. In Ghanaian culture, the way people dressed told you a lot about them, even how well educated they were. The women I watched, whether wealthy, poor, literate or illiterate—all held themselves with equal dignity.

Most were dressed in traditional wrap-around skirts printed in colorful and elaborate patterns and matching blouses. The more traditional women paired their skirts with a piece of loose fabric wrapped around the chest and draped over the left shoulder, the right shoulder left bare. It looked like a shortened version of the Roman toga. Many wore their hair in the traditional Ashanti style: very short on top and shaved all around the bottom, leaving just the sides and back very nicely cropped. The base of that hair is then colored with smooth black makeup to form a half-inch border right around the head. It's a very elegant hairstyle, and I thought as I watched these women that they looked like black sculptures, walking down the street with perfect grace.

Even the most delicate-looking were surprisingly strong, and all of them moved with an undeniable sense of purpose. The working mothers carried foodstuffs on their heads and babies on their backs. The loads atop their heads, often very high and heavy, sat precariously balanced, unaided by hands, yet swaying rhythmically in perfect unison with their body movements, like part of a well-choreographed dance. This left them with two free hands, one to hold onto a toddler and the other to wave expressively in the air as they conversed on their way to the Central Market.

Ah, the Kumasi Central Market. Now that is something else again. The whole area (approximately ten blocks wide in one direction, six blocks wide in the other) was a hive of activity, packed full of busy sweaty bodies alongside well-groomed shoppers, hawkers calling out to passers by, people selling cooked food from trays and head-mounted glass cabinets, hairdressers and barbers cutting and braiding hair whilst children weave in and out between stalls, while the musky aroma of sweet mangoes combined with the smell of fresh roasted corn on the cob in a way that can have you reaching for your purse without even bothering to haggle!

This hive has its undisputed queens—who are, in fact, known as the Produce Queens. Each queen is elected to head the various committees of buyers and sellers, and each has her own territory. The Tomato Queen, for instance, presides over a jurisdiction that includes chiles, eggplants, okras, and other vegetables with seeds; the Yam Queen, the Plantain Queen, and others control other aspects of the vegetable kingdom. One sees them all over the marketplace, arbitrating disputes and orchestrating the movement of produce around the square with the confidence and ease of well-practiced conductors. You must understand that all produce-related business transactions here take place between women; the males here work mainly as laborers, tailors, bankers, and secretaries.

Indeed, each produce committee even has its own "on-road women," who bring supplies in from rural farms to the central marketplace in a small fleet of trucks. Even before the crops are planted, the on-road women drive out to meet with the farmers, recommending that they concentrate on planting whichever crops they project will be in greatest demand at the market. Once these crops are harvested, the on-road women return to negotiate suitable bulk-buying prices, and then buy up the produce for the market's cooperatives. Upon delivery, the queens (assisted by their committees) inspect the produce and set the week's resale prices. Cheating is discouraged and punishment is meted out to anyone who surreptitiously hikes up their prices. Fair but firm, the queens are well respected by all members of the community.

All of this has remained remarkably unchanged over the years, as I recently discovered. Back home to tape a documentary segment for my television food show, I had the good fortune to interview several of the Produce Queens, some of whom have known me since I was a little girl. It had been nearly thirty years since I last saw them and they were still going strong.

Nee Yaa, the Yam Queen, whom I remember as an elder even in my childhood, was arbitrating between two women. The guilty party had been discovered on the other side of the market selling her yams at a hugely inflated price. The woman had been warned before. This time she was challenged, an argument broke out, and the errant woman was brought before the Yam Queen.

"May I remind you," Nee Yaa told her, "that the branches of any tree are only as strong as its roots, and we are the roots. We all need water, so now we've found a free-flowing source let's not be greedy. Let's share and share alike." She fined the woman and banned her from selling at the marketplace for the next two days.

Nee Yaa then turned to me and explained, "I have to cool their hearts and yet be strict." She put her arm around my shoulders and declared, "I am so glad you've returned home to roost. You see? When a bird flies around the world and its wings tire, it always finds a familiar branch to rest on."

I didn't have the heart to tell her that this time I was only there to film.

XOX ⠿ X X ⠿

Ashanti women have so much economic power; it's a shame none of that power translates into the realm of the political. This is brought out in interesting ways, as Ashanti culture is both matrilineal and polygamous, creating an odd dichotomy.

In polygamous marriages, one finds a sort of sexual roster: each wife gets to spend anywhere from one week to a month at a time doing the washing, cooking, and cleaning, and otherwise generally taking care of her husband at his place of residence. Or, if she chooses, she may stay at her family home and take care of his needs from there—except at night, when she goes to his place for their romantic trysts, leaving the baby-sitting to extended family. To this day, Ghanaian couples still don't necessarily have to cohabit, it is entirely a matter of mutual preference to do so.

I once knew a woman, a very successful seamstress, who was one of several wives married to the same man. Hers was certainly not a marriage of economic dependence; truth be known, she probably earned more money than her husband. Several weeks earlier, one of her clients had given her a beautiful pair of sandals. The seamstress carefully put the sandals away, saving them for her next week up on the sexual roster.

When her first evening with her husband finally arrived, she had high hopes for a romantic night together. She took extra care in dressing and even put on a bit of perfume. Very excited, she made her husband's favorite meal for dinner and served it to him wearing all of her finery, including her new sandals. Now, normally, as a sign of respect, a wife serves meals barefoot, but my friend was so proud of her fancy sandals that she just had to show them off to her man.

Well, the man divorced her. He was so upset that she'd worn the sandals to serve his dinner that he dismissed her without another word. As far as he was concerned, it was an unforgivable sign of disrespect.

And this in a society in which the most important person in any family is always the oldest living woman. Whether the mother, grandmother, great-aunt, or somebody of equal standing, this woman is regarded as an authority on life and hence best able to arbitrate and give advice. Even a high-ranking official would not consider making any major decision without first consulting one of the older women in his family.

Even as a child, I was upset by this state of affairs. How, I often asked myself, could men justify treating their wives as though they could not think for themselves when they were in their prime, and then turn around and treat them as sages when they rose to the position of eldest living female? But worse, I wondered, how could these capable women allow this to happen to themselves? How could this happen in a matrilineal society?

Essentially, I believe that the weakness has created the strength. That is, every African woman in a polygamous marriage knows that at any time she may be forgotten for the youth or beauty of another wife; her future is anything but secure. Ultimately, her well-being and her children's lies in her own hands. Thus, the shrewd business acumen of women like the Produce Queens.

Although there is a certain amount of competition between wives, they also realize that they are all in the same boat, and so they help each other in times of need. For instance, should one of the wives take ill, her co-wives will take over the care of her children, bring her food, and make sure that her home is looked after. But still, friendships between wives are strained, at best. Polygamy offers only a limited opportunity for deeply fulfilling emotional relationships. No matter what part of the world they are from, most females would agree that it's not easy to share your man with anywhere from three to twenty or more other women.

The solution for these women is to channel their massive capacity for love into single-minded devotion to their children. African women love their children with a ferocity that can sometimes be frightening, and with a tenderness that often brings a grown man to his knees. Everything the African woman works for is for her child; what she cannot have, she will seek to give her children.

XOX ⠿ X X ⠿

One day I stopped outside the marketplace to watch a group of mothers with their young ones. Women with nothing but a bowl or an iron bucket of water collected from the local pump will stand on the street corner in full view of everybody, washing their offspring. They line them up, two or three or five children, and scrub them with sponges made from tree bark and homemade nut-oil soap. They may be desperately poor, but their children are thoroughly clean—a clean soul, a clean spirit, and a sense of pride.

After the bath, there is only one towel to dry all the children. That done, their mother polishes them with sheer butter oil steeped in rosemary and other aromatic herbs. I watch the children glistening in the sun, standing on the street corner while one devoted woman washes and polishes each like she's polishing a precious chalice. Well, I think to myself, some people polish their silver; African women polish their children.

✕◈✕ ⠿ ✕ ✕ ⠿

When I think of the market, one of the things I think of is the wonderful food aromas that permeate it. Much market food is quite simple—roasted corn on the cob, barbecued over hot coals or just boiled in the husk and sold hot or cold. Grilled plantain served with dry-roasted peanuts. Sweet, refreshing watermelon juice. Fish and dumplings with the spicy sauces known as *shitor*. Indeed, this last dish is so popular, it has inspired a traditional folk song, "Komi ke Loo" (The Fish Song that my friends and I sang in Accra), which is sung when you eat the following recipe. *Komi* (pronounced "kormi") means corn dumpling, *ke* (pronounced "ker") is "with," and *loo* (pronounced "low") means fish or meat.

⁂ BAKED FISH ⁂

SERVES 4

3 tablespoons (1 1/3 oz/40 g) gingerroot, finely grated
4 cloves garlic, finely chopped
2 red chiles, chopped into a pulp
Salt to taste
Four fresh fillets of salmon, snapper, or tuna
2 teaspoons (5 g) butter
1 teaspoon (5 g) garlic salt

Preheat oven to 350 F (180 C). Mix together the gingerroot, garlic, chiles, and a pinch of salt, then rub this mixture all over the fillets.

Use the butter to grease four pieces of aluminum foil. Place one seasoned fillet on each, and sprinkle well with garlic salt. Loosely close the foil to form four little parcels, and bake for 20–25 minutes. Serve with dumplings and chile sauce.

✕✕ SEMOLINA DUMPLINGS ✕✕

SERVES 2-4

*(While traditionally this meal would call for cornmeal dumplings,
they cannot be made without fermented corn dough, something the average
Western kitchen isn't likely to have on hand. The semolina does
make a very nice foil for the spicy fish and shitor.)*

Salt to taste
4 cups (2 pt/1L) water
2 cups (1 lb/500 g) semolina

Salt the water and bring to a boil in a very heavy saucepan.

Pour half of the water into a second pan, and keep at a very slow boil. Add the semolina to the rest of the water on medium heat, stirring vigorously with a wooden spoon. As you stir, press the mixture against the insides of the pan, to prevent the batter from becoming lumpy.

Add small amounts of the reserved boiling water as the batter cooks, to keep it soft, stirring all the while. Continue until the batter loses some of its grittiness, softens, and cooks. Most or all of the rest of the boiling water should be used.

Remove from the pot, form into rounds the size of tennis balls, and serve alongside the fish and shitor.

I WAS NEVER HERE...

✕✕ **SHITOR** ✕✕

MAKES 4 SERVINGS

12 fresh red Thai chiles with seeds,
   finely chopped
2 medium onions, finely chopped
6 large tomatoes, blanched, peeled, and
   finely chopped
Salt to taste

Combine the chiles, onion, and tomatoes in a bowl or food processor and mash or process to a pulp. Salt to taste and serve as a sauce or salsa accompaniment.

✕✕✕ ✕✕ ✕ ✕ ✕

Another street food staple (and one that sometimes verges over into street theater) is kyinkyinga, or kebabs. These tasty skewers of meat and peppers are irresistible to flies, so the vendors keep them in glass boxes, which they balance on their heads. What a sight it is to see the vendors dashing into traffic at red lights to try and make a quick sale—balancing a heavy glass case full of hot kyinkyinga while simultaneously counting change from a money belt!

✕✕ KYINKYINGA ✕✕

SERVES 4

2 pounds (1 kg) lean steak
4 medium onions, diced
2 teaspoons (10 g) grated gingerroot
2 tablespoons (1 oz/30 g) all-purpose flour
3 oz (90 g) unsalted dry-roasted peanuts,
    ground to powder. (Use a coffee grinder or
    mortar and pestle)
2 large overripe tomatoes, blanched, peeled,
    and mashed
1 tablespoon (15 g) garlic salt
1 tablespoon (15 ml) hot sauce
1 cup (8 fl oz/250 ml) ginger wine
$^1/_2$ cup (4 fl oz/125 ml) water
3 medium green bell peppers, halved, seeded,
    and cut into one-inch (2cm) squares

Remove excess fat from meat, wipe with a clean, damp cloth or paper towel, and cut into bite-sized cubes.

In a medium bowl, mix together onions, gingerroot, flour, ⅔ of the peanut powder, tomatoes, garlic salt, and hot sauce. Set aside one half of the mixture. Combine the meat with the remaining half, mix thoroughly, and let stand at least one hour before grilling. While meat is marinating, make a sauce by adding the wine and the water to the remaining seasoning. Stir and simmer on low heat for about 5–10 minutes, stirring occasionally until the liquid reduces itself. Lower the heat.

Skewer the seasoned meat, alternating with bell-pepper squares, and grill until browned on both sides. Remove from heat, sprinkle with the remaining peanut powder, and serve with the wine sauce.

I WAS NEVER HERE...

This story is told to children to explain two of the most important factors of Ashanti life—the presence and value of the yam, one of our primary foodstuffs, and an important aspect of the matrilineal system.

※◎※ ░░ ※ ░░ HOW THE YAM ※◎※ ░░ ※ ░░
CAME TO THE ASHANT

The Ashanti have not always had yams. Indeed, in ancient times, they had none, and often found it hard to raise enough food to keep their families from being hungry, especially in the rainy season.

Then one day a traveler passed through an Ashanti village carrying many unfamiliar things, including a yam. A young man named Abu saw that yam, and realized how valuable such a thing could be to his people. He determined to find out where yams came from, and bring them back for his people.

So Abu took up his weapons and set out to find the yams. Everyone he met, he asked if they knew how to find the place where yams come from. Some people told him it was in this direction, others told him it was that way. He was beginning to despair when he came around a bend and over a hill, and there it was—fields and fields of yams growing everywhere. He asked the people working the fields where he might find the chief, and was directed to his house.

Bowing before the chief, he explained his mission. "In my country," Abu said, "there are no yams, and our people often must go hungry. If you could give me some yams to take back and plant, we wouldn't have to be hungry any more."

The chief thought about this. He said, "I must speak to my advisors." And he sent Abu to stay in his guest house while he considered.

After several days, the chief sent for Abu. He said, "I would like to help your people, but when they are no longer hungry they will become strong and they might decide to wage war against their weaker neighbors."

"This would not happen," Abu replied, "because my people are peaceful. And isn't it also true that hungry people often go to war to get food from their neighbors?"

"True," said the chief, "but I may still be risking a great deal if I help you. I will only feel secure in giving you the yams if you will bring me a man from your tribe to live here as a hostage."

So Abu returned to Ashanti and told his father of his journey. He finished by saying, "Father, you have many sons. Why not send one of them as a hostage to the yam chief and then we will have yams and our people will never go hungry again."

But Abu's father could not bring himself to send any of his sons into exile. So Abu went next to his brothers, and told them of the yam chief's offer. He asked each of them to send one of their sons as hostage and each of them in turn refused.

In desperation, Abu returned to the yam country, and told the chief that he couldn't find anyone to act as a hostage. He asked if there was anything else that he could do, but the chief only shook his head. "I'm sorry," he replied, "but I can't give you the yams without security."

Abu returned home in sorrow, for he saw no solution. But when he reached his village, he suddenly remembered his sister, who also had a son. He ran to her house and poured out his story. She listened, then said, "But I have only this one son. If he should go, I will have none."

"Then we are lost," said Abu. "You were my last hope. Our people are doomed to go hungry." Seeing his sorrow, his sister asked him to explain again about the yams, and how they could save their people. Finally, she agreed to send her son after all, for she saw how important it could be to Ashanti.

When Abu returned from the yam country this time, he brought yams for his people to plant. Soon the yams grew and were harvested, and from that day forth, there was always plenty to eat in Ashanti.

As for Abu, he decried his father and brothers for refusing to send their sons to the yam country. "From now on," he said, "I will have nothing more to do with them. Only my sister was willing to risk a son to save our people from hunger, and she must be honored for this. When I die, all of my property will be given to my nephew, who is now living in the yam country, for he is the one who made it possible for us to conquer hunger."

And so it was that many years hence, when Abu died an old and rich man, his cattle and his land passed not to his sons or brothers, but to his nephew, his sister's son. And the people of Ashanti, to honor Abu for bringing them the yam, which had since become one of their most vital crops, declared that all Ashanti would follow Abu's lead.

And from that time onward, when a man dies, he leaves everything he owns to his sister's son. And further, in honor of Abu, the Ashanti people refer to families as *abusua*, and borrowed money is *bosea (from abu-sea)*, or "borrowed from Abu."

And to this day, boys inherit their property not from their fathers, as is the case in other lands, but from their mother's brothers, just like Abu's nephew.

Fields of Vision

Grandpa was my father's father. Before he was struck blind, he had been the captain of a ship. Apparently he had contracted river blindness, onchocerciasis, on a run with some merchants up through the interior of the Congo.

I used to visit him during my holidays in Accra, and during the short time that we lived there. Throughout my childhood, I had a sort of an aversion to old people, except for my mum's Mum, Grandma Emma. I don't know why I didn't like them—they all spoiled me rotten—but they smelled funny and their wrinkled faces scared me. I felt as though, being closer to death, they carried a spirit that could jump into my soul and carry me away.

And there was something else about Grandpa that bothered me: even though he was supposedly blind, he always kept his eyes open. By the time I reached the age of six or so, this had come to be a real thorn in my side. Six-year-old logic told me that if he was *really* blind, his eyes would be closed. So, I concluded, the old man must be fooling around to get everybody's sympathy. My suspicions were only confirmed by the fact that he found his way around his house so easily, never bumping into any chairs or walls. No doubt about it, Grandpa was a fraud, and I was determined to expose him. Then everybody would see him as I did—mean and wrinkled and definitely not honest.

One afternoon when Grandpa was sitting in the outside yard with my dad and a few other relatives, I decided to prove my point. Very quietly, I nipped into the house and began rearranging the furniture. I may have been little, but I was also determined, and I pulled and tugged and heaved and shoved and finally managed to move the furniture into awkward places. The piece that I worked the hardest on moving was his favorite chair, a large high-backed wicker rocker that he kept by one of the windows so he could sit and enjoy the fresh sea breezes while listening to the sounds of life outside. I moved that chair far, far away from the window and replaced it with a traditional little stool.

After about an hour I heard the old man asking for me. "Where is Naa Tsenkua Charity?" He always insisted on adding the "Charity." He was the only one who called me that, and I hated it, because I got teased about that name all through school. I think it had been the name of my father's twin sister, who had drowned when they were children.

"Where is Naa Tsenkua Charity?" he called again.

I answered, "In here, Grandpa."

He came into the house, and headed straight for his favorite chair by the window. He was so sure that it would be there, as it always was, that he didn't bother to check. Instead, as he had a thousand times before, he put his hands behind him to grab hold of the sides, let his weight go, and leaned back to sit down. This time, however, unlike all those other times, he landed painfully and awkwardly on the stool, which tipped backwards and sent him crashing flat on his back. The old man couldn't even scream, he was in so much pain.

My father and the rest of the family outside heard the crash, followed by me screaming, "Grandpa's fallen! Grandpa's fallen!"

I was expecting to be beaten black and blue. But when everyone rushed in, they were too busy trying to put the poor old man together to even notice me in the corner of the room, cowering with fear.

Then someone realized what had happened. "Who shifted the chair?" they asked. "Grandpa's chair has always been at the window. Who shifted it?"

My grownup cousin Nicho looked around and found the chair sitting on the far side of the room. As she went to retrieve it, she finally saw me in the corner, trying to make myself invisible. "What are you doing sitting down there?" she snapped. "Get up and come help Grandpa. Move the stool."

Instead of just moving the stool, I decided I had to make everything right, right then. I sped around the room trying to push everything back to where it belonged. Cousin Nicho looked at me strangely, as did my father, but nobody said anything just then.

The old man couldn't sit up in his chair; he'd really damaged his back. Four of the men, including my father, carried him to his bed and they sent for the doctor. (At that time my father was still a nurse and, even if he had been qualified to treat his father, I doubt if he would have considered it ethical.)

Once Grandpa was out of danger, my father called me to him. Gruffly.

I knew I was in trouble, but I went to him just the same. Daddy picked me up and sat me on his knee; sitting on his knee normally meant nice, kind things, but the voice in which he called me meant horrible, mean things. So my emotions were mixed.

My father grabbed my ears. This was part of his way of punishing us: he never hit us, but he'd been working in the operating room for so long, and scrubbing his hands with antiseptics and hard brushes, that the skin of his palms was very rough. So it was like having your earlobes wrapped in sandpaper.

He turned me to look at him and he said, "Why did you do it?"

I WAS NEVER HERE…

He didn't say, "Did you do it? Was it you?" He just knew and said, "Why did you do it?"

I broke down in tears and confessed: "Because I thought Grandpa was lying, his eyes are always open. How can he be blind if his eyes are still open?"

My father answered in a very calm voice, almost gentle, "You've learnt an important lesson today, Naa Tsenkua. Blind people can have their eyes open. "Being blind" he said, and I have never forgotten it, "being blind is not just a physical thing. Sometimes it can be a blindness of the spirit or a blindness of the emotions."

I was too young at the time to fully understand what he was saying, but I listened carefully as he continued, "Grandpa's blindness is physical. He doesn't need to have his eyes closed, because inside the eyeball itself is where the trouble is. That's why he can't see. But you, Naa Tsenkua, you are yourself blind too; you were spiritually blind for not being able to feel for your Grandpa. And now you are emotionally blind because you are ashamed of yourself for what you've done. Now you must go in there and admit to Grandpa that you did it and ask his forgiveness."

"I'm very, very sorry," I said, and I couldn't stop crying. When I went into Grandpa's room, he was lying there with his eyes closed. I called out, "Grandpa, are you dead?"

He laughed a very little and he winced as he laughed, "No, I am not dead. Is that you Naa Tsenkua Charity?"

"Yes, Grandpa."

"Why did you do it?"

He knew too! "Grandpa, I'm sorry," I said, hiccuping with tears.

"Come here, Naa Tsenkua Charity, come here and sit on the bed. I can't sit up and cuddle you like I usually do, but sit on the bed and hold my hand. Let me feel you." Still with his eyes closed, he groped for my hand on the edge of the bed. "Give me your hands." With his one hand, he held both of mine. He said, "I'm not mad at you, little one, but please don't do it again. I will mend." He squeezed my hands gently. "I might be old, but I'm strong. I am made of stern stuff. I will mend."

I was shocked and filled with emotion; here this old man, whom I had seen as wrinkled and mean, was being so kind to me after I had hurt him terribly. Through all my tears and apologies, I made a solemn promise to myself and to my Grandpa. With all the sincerity of youth, I swore, "When I grow up, I will make up for this; I will help all the blind people of the world."

Of course, that was a promise I couldn't keep. But I did train as an ophthalmic nurse, and worked for several years as a dispensing optician, and the one charity that I consistently support is the Royal Society for the Blind. Still, I haven't made it up to Grandpa yet, not fully, not yet.

While I no longer work in the "field of vision," I spend an awful lot of time in the public eye. Often during interviews, I am asked, "So, what is a dispensing optician doing in the performing arts?"

My only answer is, "I am here because there are still so many shortsighted people around." I hope, with my work, to open eyes.

Hunger Go to Sleep

A West African childhood, at least for me, meant a kaleidoscope of color and a cacophony of sound, a mixture of happy laughter and sometimes abject misery. I remember births and deaths, oil lamps flickering in the night, the sweet aroma of crispy fried plantain. I remember running with my cousins to hide from the ancestral spirits buried in the vaults behind the walls of our family home, and watching the legs of people passing in front of the four-poster wooden beds under which we hid, whispering and giggling, trying to guess which legs belonged to the living and which to ghosts chasing us from the spirit world. But most of all, I remember the ceremonies we were privileged to witness.

For the Ga people, August in Accra is a vibrant month, filled with celebration, feasting, and cultural pride, culminating in the annual Homowo Festival.

Literally translated, Homowo means "hunger go to sleep," and it's shouted all during the festival as people parade through the streets, sprinkling steamed, unleavened cornmeal everywhere. Legend has it that the festival began in ancient days, after the Ga tribe suffered a terrible famine while migrating from western Nigeria to their present location in southern Ghana. Miraculously, the year following the famine, the Ga experienced a bumper harvest of fish. Ever since then, the people have celebrated this blessing with colorful processions, traditional song and dance, and ritual meals centered around fish in palm nut soup and unleavened cornmeal.

The Homowo Festival has always sparked my sense of adventure. It is a time of joy, of plenty, of singing and dancing in the streets and eating until you're so full you can't even move. As an adventurous child, I particularly loved exploring what went on behind the scenes and, of all the ceremonies I witnessed, my all-time favorite remains the Twins Festival.

To understand this, you must know that throughout West Africa, the birth of twins is considered to be a supernatural occurrence. The twins themselves are considered to be magical beings who have both earthly and spiritual presence, but, for the most part, are believed to share a single spirit.

While I'm not sure exactly why this is, it is interesting to note that studies have proven that West Africans can rightfully claim the highest incidence of twin births in the world. But having twins is not in itself enough to bring good luck. Indeed, to avoid bringing bad luck to the rest of the family, parents are obliged to have three more children *after* the twins. This is not so bad for those parents whose first pregnancy results in a set of twins, but God help the poor mother who already has three previous children! She will still be expected to go the full distance. Some such parents find the prospect of further children so economically daunting that they'd much prefer to risk the wrath of the gods. And this is becoming increasingly so as people leave behind the old beliefs.

XOX ≡ X X ≡

One morning when I was about ten, my cousin Naa Deedei (Miranda) and I decided to spy on the preparations for the Twins Festival. We snuck out just after dawn, before Miranda's mother, Aunty Chris, could wake up to tell us we weren't allowed to go. The chickens and roosters in the yard set up an awful chorus of cackling and crowing as we tiptoed through them, but somehow we got away undetected by anyone else.

Down the lane and two houses later, we joined three other inquisitive children outside the nearest household blessed with twins. Peering through holes in the dilapidated outer walls of the yard, we watched two older women washing the identical twin girls in preparation for the day's ritual. As the house had no bathroom, they had to bathe the girls early before everyone else arose. (Other members of the family would be going to the big public bathhouse later to wash.)

Even earlier, the fetish priestess had been by to pour a libation at the twins' shrine (most traditional houses with twins have a small shrine somewhere in the house or backyard), and leave magical leaves for the washing ceremony. This libation is supposed to honor and appease the twins' magical spirit, but apparently it hadn't worked because a fight soon broke out over the soap, the naked twins pelting each other with water and leaves. Any other day, these squabbling eleven-year-olds would be chastised, but not today.

The fight over, the twins allowed their relatives to finish washing them. After the bath, the women dried the twins, cleaned and trimmed their nails, then polished their skins with sheer butter (nkutoh) until they gleamed like precious jewelry.

At the other end of the yard, a drummer was already up, painting red, yellow and green stripes around the outside of his big drum. Periodically, he drummed out a few notes, adding to the feeling of expectancy and excitement in the air. Miranda voiced her opinion that the drummer must have woken up early to get a good look at the

Dorinda, age 10, in Kumasi

girls, in case he wanted to marry one or both of them when they turned sixteen.

An older boy who was watching with us pushed Miranda and said, "He's their dad, you fool!"

We all giggled. Poor Miranda, she never meant any harm. I gave her a reassuring hug.

I WAS NEVER HERE...

By the time we refocussed our attention on them, the twins were totally covered from head to toe in *ayilor*, the traditional white tribal clay. They looked like ghosts. What a waste, I thought, and after all that polishing, too.

The clay was followed by ritual dressing in white clothes and a special breakfast of boiled eggs on top of *oto* (mashed yam colored with palm oil) and a glass of cold water each.

By now it was mid morning and the twins had become impatient with all the fussing. They ran to open their gates, eager to go out and play. We didn't want them to know we'd been watching them, so Miranda quickly grabbed a rock and drew a hopscotch cross in the dirt road, and we began playing fervently, as if we'd been at it all morning. The twins came over and asked if we wanted to go with them to find enough people to play *Aso*, a group rhythm game that can last for hours. As we followed them to the town square, I realized that the white clay on their skin smelled like chalk, reminding me of school.

All over the district, small groups of children were already outside playing and shrieking with pleasure. Each group of dark little bodies was sprinkled with pairs of ghostly white twins, vying to be the center of attention. The playing went on like this, punctuated by snacks from vendors, until an hour or so before sundown, when we knew that all the twins would have to return home for the highlight of the Twins Festival.

We followed our set of twins back to their house, where the fetish priestess was waiting for them at their shrine, accompanied by two other priestesses carrying sacred magical garlands made of twisted vines and leaves. Since the night before, the priestess had been soaking magic leaves in a bucket of water in a corner of the backyard. Now that part of the leaves had been used, she transferred the remaining leaves and sacred water into two identical, deep white-enamel bowls and added more leaves along with silver coins. The older boy told us that this bowl of coins and water is called "tsésé" (pronounced chay-say), and explained that each set of twins has their own special fetish priest or priestess, depending on their gender, to take charge of the formalities and the happiness of the twins' spirit.

As soon as the twins arrived home, relatives, neighbors, and inquisitive onlookers both outside and in the backyard began clapping and singing the special Twins Song, using a combination of the twins' real and spirit names to praise them individually and the virtues of twins in general. Slowly, as if possessed, the high priestess advanced towards the twins, chanting invocations. She deliberately and carefully placed a magical garland around each one's neck, upon which the twins suddenly began to convulse uncontrollably, clearly in a trance-like state.

Aided by family members and the other priestesses the high priestess placed a bowl full of magical leaves, water, and silver coins on each twin's head. Without ceasing their gyrations, the twins raised their arms up and clutched the bowls. Their eyes looked vacant and glazed, no longer recognizing family or friends; the only person able to reach through their trance was the high priestess. Finally, the seemingly possessed twins charged through the gates of their house with younger friends and family following to make sure they didn't hurt themselves.

Excited, Miranda and I joined the crowd.

The high priestess and her attendants followed at a more leisurely pace. Indeed, they did not need to hurry, as they were apparently able to call the gyrating twins to a halt at any given moment using a few magical chants. After one such call, the priestess walked up to the twins, picked a few wet leaves from the bowls, and sprinkled the crowds with the water to bless them. As soon as she finished, the twins started moving again. The high priestess invited members of the public to throw more silver coins into the tsésé, precariously balanced on top of the twins' heads. It is quite a feat to get your coins into the moving bowls, but those who do are guaranteed good fortune throughout the following year. I was too short to try, but the older boy tossed some coins in for me and Miranda.

As the twins led us through town, more and more people joined the parade calling out praises and encouragement. The streets were brimming with throngs of people following other twins, calling out to them, asking them questions. Sometimes the twins answered in the voice of their spirit, other times they didn't answer at all. It is an amazing sight; as far as the eye can see are different sets of twins carrying white-enamel bowls on their heads, totally out of it, possessed, gyrating forwards backwards and sideways, running in different directions. And I was caught in the middle of this mad choreography, a dangerous sea of hot human lava, and me too excited to worry.

Although the streets were absolutely full, the crowds parted like magic whenever the twins wanted to get through. This is because everyone knows that evil might come to you if you stand in the way of these spirits. From time to time our group broke into the Twins Song and everybody joined in joyously. A few people brought the odd drum, but they are not allowed to do full drumming, just a simple beat to enhance the spirits' movements for the twins.

Our procession passed various hawkers trying to sell us food from their stalls, or charcoal piled into mounds on the side of the road. Miranda and I passed hungrily by a stand selling rice and stew wrapped in a big leaf, but dared not stop to eat, for fear of being left behind. Instead, we quickly bought some roasted plantain and a couple of drinks from a hawker along the way, gulping them down as we ran to catch up with our group. With the fires, the food, and the shouts, it felt like a street carnival and I didn't want to miss a minute.

After much walking, the twins eventually led us to a grassy verge on the outskirts of the district. In unison, as though ordered, they finally tipped their bowls over, coins and all, in a watery offering to the grass, and promptly fell to the ground in an exhausted heap.

The high priestess walked right past me on her way to attend to them. This was the first time I had ever seen her close up—I'd always been too scared to really look at her, having heard that fetish priests will take your spirit away if you look them in the eyes. For the first time, I really looked at her, not eyeball to eyeball, just kind of checking her out. I noticed that she had a healthy mustache, the kind of hair I saw Dad shaving off every morning, and for some reason this convinced me that she was as powerful as everyone said. She walked up to the twins, leaned in over them, and broke into an ear-piercing chant. It was her final prayer for the collapsed twins.

They looked up at her, focused for the first time in hours, and blinked several times. A truck passed by and they turned sharply in its direction. Clearly they had returned; they could hear ordinary things again. "What are we doing here?" they asked, bewildered, and everybody tried to answer at once as several people helped the twins to their feet.

I became aware that I was still holding onto Miranda's hand. We turned to stare at each other, silently acknowledging the spectacle we had just witnessed. We smiled spontaneously and I hooked my arm through hers. Everybody else looked tired, and the moon was just beginning to peer out from behind the evening clouds. Some children started singing the Moon Song and, grateful for the release, I joined in the singing as we began the long, slow journey home.

THE MOON SONG

Nyontsélé ni edze wo ba shwèè wo ba gboo
Moon which has appeared, we will play till we drop

Nyontsélé ni edze wo ba shwèè wo ba gboo
Moon which has appeared, we will play till we drop

Nyontsélé ni edze wo ba shwèè wo ba gboo
Moon which has appeared, we will play till we drop

Nyontsélé ni edze wo ba shwèè wo ba gboo
Moon which has appeared, we will play till we drop

Nkèè Nyontsélé ni edzeee, Nyontsélé niedzeee
I say the Moon which has appeared means we can play till we drop

Nyontsélé ni edze wo ba shwèè wo ba gboo
I say the Moon which has appeared means we can play till we drop

Nyontsélé ni edze wo ba shwèè wo ba gboo
   wo ba shwèè shwèè shwèè wo ba gboo
   wo ba shwèè shwèè shwèè wo ba gboo
Moon which has appeared, we will play till we drop
   we will play, play, play, till we drop
   we will play, play, play, till we drop

THE TWINS' SONG

TWINS' SONG (FEMALES)

Yee ye yee ye yee

Akwéle Suma	Yee yeyee yeyee
Akuorkor Omaso	Yee yeyee yeyee
Tawia Apiajei	Yee yeyee yeyee
Nyankoma Ago	Yee yeyee yeyee
Abam Hèlè	Yee yeyee yeyee

(These are tribal names, followed by a yee yeyee!)

Mitee Langmali, Miyana Wuoko
When I went to Langmali, I saw some chicken

Mina wuo mijofoi, Mijoofoi aahu etor mi
When I saw the chicken I ran away, I ran so much I got exhausted

Etor mi aahu nkortso
I was so exhausted I climbed a tree

Nkwortso aahu nkplékéʃi
I climbed a tree so much that I came down again

Nkplékéʃi Akwélé
Nkplékéʃi Akuorkor
I descended for Akwele, I descended for Akuorkor

TWINS' SONG (MALES)

Awo, awo, awo awoo

Oko Nipa	Awo awo-awoo, Awo
Akuertè Okulu	Awo awo-awoo, Awo
Tawia Apiajei	Awo awo-awoo, Awo
Nyankuma Ago	Awo awo-awoo, Awo
Abam Hèlè	Awo awo-awoo, Awo

(These are tribal names followed by Awo awo awoo!)

PARENTS OF TWINS

Sikatsèmei ntao ablékuma   Amenaa!
Rich folks want blessings   but can't have it

Adiagbatsèmei ntao ablékuma   Amenaa!
The well-to-do want blessings   but can't have it

Korlitsèmei ntao ablékuma   Amenaa!
Wearers of beautiful korli beads want blessings but can't have it

Ablékuma, ebakuma ngmaibi
Ngmaibi O, Yeyee!
Ngmaibi O, Yeyee!
O ye yee!

(repeat entire song from beginning)

Here are recipes for some of the dishes we feasted on during the Homowo festival. They will indeed put anyone's hunger most deliciously to sleep!

⚒⚒ FRIED PLANTAIN ⚒⚒

SERVES 2

1 large plantain, very ripe but not too soft
Salt to taste
Vegetable oil for frying (corn oil works well)
2 tablespoons (2 oz/40 g) brown sugar
1 teaspoon (5 g) grated nutmeg

Peel the plantain and slice diagonally into four pieces. Rub salt all over these slices.

Heat oil in a deep nonstick frying pan until the oil starts to smoke lightly. Carefully lower the plantain pieces into the hot oil and fry, turning regularly, until they are browned all over.

Remove the cooked plantains from oil and place on absorbent paper to drain. To serve, place two slices on a plate and sprinkle with sugar. Serve hot topped with nutmeg or modern additions: ice cream, whipped cream, or sour cream.

⚒⚒⚒⚒ ⚒ ⚒ ⚒⚒

The next recipe calls for soured, or fermented cornmeal. Mix the meal into a paste with cold water, cover it, and allow it to stand for 2-3 days. When it starts to ferment, it acquires a light fuzz on top. Clean off the fuzzy top and use the fermented corn dough beneath.

✖✖ **KPOKPOI** ✖✖
STEAMED CORNMEAL

SERVES 2

Muslin or fresh corn husks (about 10 to 12 leaves)
2 cups (1 lb/500 g) soured white cornmeal
1 cup (8 oz/250 g) thick mashed potatoes or
thick paste of corn dough (partly steamed
to make it thick and sticky)
8 okras
$^{1}/_{2}$ cup (4 fl oz/125 ml) palm oil
2 medium onions, peeled and finely chopped

Position a clay steamer (or metal, if clay is not available) over a pot of boiling water. Carefully line the inside of the steamer with muslin or fresh corn husks, being sure to cover it thoroughly, then sprinkle with the soured cornmeal. Seal around the base of the steamer, where it meets the pot, with the mashed potatoes or sticky corn dough. Cover and allow the cornmeal to steam until the grains swell and become slightly sticky (they may also turn a pastel yellow).

While the cornmeal is steaming, boil the okra in salted water. When cooked, drain and set four of them aside for decoration. Mash the other four.

Melt the palm oil and fry the onions until lightly browned. Do not drain.

By this time, the cornmeal should be cooked. Remove from heat and separate the grains using two forks. You can also push it through a sieve to separate (use a wooden spoon for this.)

Drain off about half the palm oil, depending on how oily you like your food (some people use all of the oil; it's a matter of personal preference), then add the oil, onion, and mashed okra, and mix thoroughly.

Serve in a dish garnished with the remaining okra, along with Palmnut Soup (see recipe page 36).

O nce there was a little boy who was born very, very tiny. His mum and dad had been waiting to have a child for a long time, so when they saw that their son was healthy they were overjoyed. They didn't care that he weighed no more than a sweet potato, and they didn't care that he was as bald as a melon, they couldn't have loved him more. They named him Kofi Baako, meaning firstborn.

As the little boy grew, his parents began to notice that he didn't talk as the other children did. He had no trouble at all communicating with the birds that flew around their hut, and the cows seemed to understand him just fine, but he would not, or could not, speak the language of humans. This caused his parents some mild concern, but they loved him just the same and didn't let it bother them too much.

No sooner was the boy four years old than the father began taking him out to the paddocks and fields to learn how to tend the goats.

Every day before they left, the mother would say, "Kofi, please be careful. I know the goats like to eat the tall grass, but snakes like the tall grass, too. They like to hide in it and wait for their next meal."

But Kofi never took any notice of his mother. He thought she fussed over him far too much, and he rather liked going off with his father and pretending to be a man.

The mother never said anything more, but she worried. Every day when she watched them leave, she would look up to the skies and pray that the boy and his father would at all times be protected by the ancestral spirits, who watch over us in the form of stars. And she prayed that one day the boy would come to understand just how much his mother loved him.

By the age of seven, Kofi had still not learned to talk. One day it occurred to his father that perhaps Kofi might be lonely, so he decided to find him a friend. The very next week, one of the nanny goats died in childbirth, leaving her twin kids as orphans. Kofi's father gave the baby goats to his son; Kofi now had not one, but two friends.

Kofi was very happy. He fussed over his baby goats from morning till night. Now this is the same boy who hated it when his mother fussed over *him*, but he didn't see the similarity. After all, it was obvious that his little goats needed protection and guidance. And he was a very good friend to them. He not only taught them to speak goat language, but he tried to teach them other languages as well. He would do bird calls, or pretend to be a duck, he would moo like a cow or bray like a donkey; the little kids never did master any of these other languages, but they would skip and play around him as he tried, perfectly content.

One day all the goats were together, chewing the tall grass, while Kofi watched from a distance. Suddenly he heard a rustling and saw a movement in the grass. He looked carefully, and to his great horror, what did he see but a young python slithering towards the herd of goats, and heading straight for his baby kids. Had his mother not warned him about playing in the tall grass? But he had never once taken any notice. His father walked in the tall grass any time he pleased, so Kofi had naturally figured that he could do the same.

Now he jumped up and down, calling to the goats to warn them. He first made his goat call, and when that didn't work he tried his cow call and his donkey call, and when the twin kids still ignored him, he tried his bird calls. He even hit the ground with his feet, imitating the foot-stomping dance of the billy goat in his father's paddocks. But either his two little charges were too far away to hear, or they were choosing to ignore him. Kofi couldn't bear to see the python swallow his baby goats, so finally, in desperation, he ran straight into the path of the python and grabbed the two babies, a struggling kid under each of his small arms. And then he froze, as the

python swayed and focused, ready to strike.

Now his mother, who just happened to be passing by on her way back from the river also spotted this scene. Without a second thought, she ran to save her son, arriving just in time to tip a huge jar of water over onto the snake, just before it struck at Kofi and the goats. The water jar landed on the python's head, trapping him within.

Kofi could see the python's thick tail thrashing about and twirling behind his mother as she sat proudly on top of her jar. He rushed to her, the baby goats still clutched in his arms. Kofi looked into his mother's eyes, a silent grateful apology.

"Remember this day, son," said Kofi's mother, "for what you are, I have been, and what I am, you will be."

✕◇✕ ░░░ ✕ ✕ ░░░

This was one of my grandmother's favorite sayings. Whenever I became too sassy, she'd say "Remember child, what you are I have been and what I am, you will be!"

Hundred Pounds Double Bass

If brains were any indication of size, Beth Cudjoe would have been a giant. Instead, she was a diminutive powerhouse of intelligence and mischief, with an irreverent, wicked sense of humor that matched my own. She was ten, I was nine, and the mutual attraction was instant. We became inseparable. Now, a year later, our friendship continued to blossom.

Beth was a fair-skinned black girl, which earned her the nickname "Red," and had one rather peculiar physical trait: her head was shaped like a corned-beef tin. Narrow at the back, it tapered outward and forward to form her face. This may sound odd, but I don't mean it as an insult. It's just that I had ample time to observe that head as I sat behind it during exams in Standard Two (sixth grade), willing myself to psychically absorb the information contained within. Best friends or no, Red and I declared intellectual war come exam times, and she was a formidable opponent. She would beat me at arithmetic, I would prevail in English. She would take top marks in history; I'd beat her in geography. From term to term, we vied for first place in the class.

Head shape aside, Red was really a very pretty girl, with a shock of loose, curly black hair and very full black lips that always looked as though she'd just applied black lipstick to them. She had lovely white teeth, and when she smiled kids and adults alike were dazzled. In short, Red was cute, astute, knew it and used it like a weapon—mercilessly.

We had English first, followed by geography, art, and arithmetic before lunch. One fateful day, Red and I decided to skip out of school and have an adventure. We already knew most of the lessons for the morning, and felt that since we were so far ahead of everyone else, we could afford a break. Red lived right smack in the middle of our local red-light district, just a couple of miles down the road from our school. And while we weren't exactly sure what prostitutes did, being pretty naive about sexual matters at that age, we admired them as street theater and wanted to check them out close up. As an adult, I realize how dangerous our little jaunt could have been, but at the time, it felt like just another chance to show off my performance skills.

Red's mother worked during the day and her father had died before she was born, so we knew we could use her home as a base of operations. We put our plan into action. First, Red requested permission to go to the toilet. I waited for my chance, which came soon enough.

"Exercise books, pencils, and reading books out," the teacher announced. "Today we are going to read the story of Shogologo Bankoshi." As she turned to write this on the board, I asked if I, too, could be excused to use the toilet. She didn't even turn around to see who was asking—my big, gravelly voice always gave me away. Indeed, it had earned me my first nickname, "Double Bass." My clothes had earned me a second nickname, "Hundred Pounds." This came about on the first day of school when, with the uninhibited garrulousness of youth, I let slip the cost of my pricey new outfit. Of course, I neglected to mention to my very impressed classmates that my mother had purchased the outfit on sale for a fraction of that original price. So, from that day onwards, throughout my three-year stint at Yaa

Achia Girls School, I was known as Hundred Pounds Double Bass.

Red met me outside the school gates and we practically danced to her house, elated that it had been so easy to escape. We figured we had about two or three hours of fun before we had to get back to school. We bought ice-cream bars from a vendor with a freezer box mounted on the front of his bicycle. It tasted of powdered milk and dyed our lips purple and orange, but we didn't care. We were free!

When we reached Red's immaculate apartment, she immediately produced an assortment of clothes and wigs from her mother's closet. Luckily for us Mrs. Cudjoe was as petite as her daughter, and we were able to wear her blouses without too much adjusting. Likewise with the wigs—Red wore a loose Afro curl, I chose a short straight bob with bangs. The skirts were more problematic, as they were like tents on us and, of course, we wanted them as tight-fitting as possible, but a handful of safety pins and a little mischief can do wonders.

After about an hour of tucking, plucking, pinning, padding, and brushing, we almost looked the part—frilly red and pink blouses buttoned over padded bras and matched with sleek, knee-length black skirts. Now for the makeup! We set to on Mrs. Cudjoe's pancake foundation, lipsticks, liquid eyeliner, eye shadow, false eyelashes, and eyebrow pencils, quickly transforming ourselves into proper street ladies. We must have been a real sight, but we thought we looked beautiful. We checked ourselves in the mirror, took one last look out the window at our professional counterparts below and, throwing long chiffon scarves around our necks, we carefully descended to the street—still wearing our school shoes. None of Mrs. Cudjoe's high heels came anywhere near fitting us.

Our appearance nearly caused a car accident, and did, in fact, create a traffic jam! It seemed as though every taxi driver and private-car chauffeur had eyes only for us. We were thrilled—and uncertain as to quite how to proceed. We planned to stick together and watch how the pros worked. And work they did! We watched them walk up to a rolled-down car window, chat a bit with the occupant, then get in and drive off with him. Or, they would take money from the driver and wait for him to park, after which they'd disappear together into one of the nearby buildings.

Unlike the drivers, the street ladies were not happy to see us. One by one, they came up and told us off—nicely at first, then more and more aggressively. But none of their abuse worked to scare us off, because we were already petrified—frozen to our spot on the corner under Mrs. Cudjoe's windows. So, they started offering us money to leave. This was intriguing, but we weren't sure how to react. Were we going to have to go into one of those buildings with them, like they did when car drivers gave them money? We were still trying to decide what to do about our first bribe, of three pounds, when a big woman with a younger, prettier woman on her arm walked up, thrust five pounds into my hand, and told us to beat it off her turf. Red and I were incredulous. The nerve! This was Red's street, she'd lived there all her life.

I decided that the poor woman and her friend were probably out of their minds. The way they looked, I didn't see how they could have owned much of anything, let alone the corner we were standing on. After all, they were both dressed in *obroni waawu*. While this is the term for second-hand clothes, the literal translation is "whiteman dead." The basic impression, that one wouldn't own these clothes until a white person had passed away and left them, meant that wearing obroni waawu was looked down upon and no one would ever admit to wearing them, even if most people had at one time or another.

What, I whispered to Red, made these crazy women think that they could kick us off our corner when we were wearing Mrs. Cudjoe's good clothes and they only had obroni waawu? I told her to remind them of this, but instead heard her say, "Well, you'll have to give us more money than this or we'll just stay here all day."

I nearly dropped dead of fright as the big woman moved in very

I WAS NEVER HERE...

close to us and, looking carefully around, reached slowly into the bosom of her dress. I was sure she was going for a knife, but instead she retrieved and handed over another five pounds.

"Now get out of here you little root rats," she bellowed, "before I kill you both."

We grabbed the money and ran all the way up the stairs back to Red's apartment, where we fell onto the couch breathless but ecstatic. We had made thirteen pounds in less than an hour—not bad for two kids under eleven!

We tidied up, got back into our own clothes, and then set out to spend our loot. Holding hands, we ran back downstairs and into the alley behind Red's house where vendors sold all sorts of candies, confections, and sweet drinks that we were never allowed to have. We ate our treats in Red's living room, watching our "friends" the pros working the streets below and giggling at their antics. We imitated their walks and mannerisms, and laid bets on which ones we thought would get picked up the most. Eventually, we ate and drank ourselves into a stupor, waking with a start to the sound of screeching car tires. It was three o'clock; school would be finished for the day in twenty minutes! We brushed down our uniforms, faces, and hair, and raced back to school, arriving just as the kids were pouring out of the gates. Nobody noticed us, and we were able to sneak up the back steps and retrieve our schoolbags.

It wasn't until I was walking home that I had the amusing thought that if anyone had asked me my name I would have replied "Hundred Pounds...." Would they have realized that was my name, not my price?

XOX ⸻ X X ⸻

Mum was waiting for me when I got home. Our district was finally getting electricity, and workmen had been wiring up houses all week, so things were a bit messy, but she seemed downright chirpy. I said hello to her, and to my grandma and Aunty Betty, then went to get a cool drink. Mum called in to the kitchen, asking me to fetch her slippers from the bedroom. As I entered the bedroom, she followed me in and locked the door behind her.

In one quick movement, she grabbed the front of my uniform and pulled me toward her, asking, "How was school today?" I remember thinking that her hold on me was a trifle aggressive for such an innocent question. I looked up at her, and suddenly got that awful feeling you only get when you've done something wrong and you know you're done for—that the only question remaining, really, is what your punishment will be, and how painful.

I looked into Mum's eyes with the optimism only a child can have, looking for a glimmer of hope, however small, that I was not in fact about to be thrashed to death. I couldn't read her, but figuring that since I had only just arrived home myself, there was no way she could have learned of my little escapade, I felt it was worth the risk. "Oh, school was fine," I said, noncommittally.

She continued, "So, did you do anything interesting in English today?" Ah! The opening I'd been hoping for. I perked up, and with a half-hearted smile, said, "Yes Mum, we read Shogologo Bankooshi."

She let go of me momentarily, lulling me into a false sense of security. But it had only been to grab a long piece of electrical wire, no doubt left behind by the workmen. Lashing out at me with it, she shouted, "Why do you lie to me? Where were you all day? My patients tell me you've been seen in Odum, amongst the prostitutes. Do I send you to school to sell your body? Have you no self-respect? Are you even my child, or some devil sent to try me?"

The chastisement and beating continued as I screamed and ran around the cramped, crowded bedroom with Mum in pursuit. Finally, I realized that I couldn't get away from her because she'd locked the door, so I stopped running. But Mum interpreted this as further defiance and intensified her attack on me, still using the electrical wire. By now I had screamed myself hoarse, so I just stood stupefied as she flailed away on me.

At some point, I became aware that my grandma and Aunty Betty were pounding on the bedroom door, imploring Mum to leave me alone and let them in. They threatened to report her to my dad and to the family elders, but she took no notice. Indeed, she kept on beating me until she was totally out of breath, her rage finally expended. There was a rustle of fabric as my mother's purple and green skirt brushed past my head. I lay curled up on the floor long after she left the room; this beating had reached my soul. Indeed, until I was thirty-five years old, the colors purple and green together made me ill. It wasn't until recently that I realized why.

My grandmother and aunt took care of me. I remember being lifted up, and the cool sheets of my bed; the smell of Florida water perfume and the sting of warm water and iodine. I fell into a deep, sad sleep.

The whole family ostracized my mother for weeks.

XOX ===== X X =====

I understand now that my mother was afraid of what might become of me, but the punishment was so outlandishly disproportionate. Essentially, she found it unthinkable that her precious daughter was associating with prostitutes, even in jest, so she decided to beat any such urges out of me. For years I hated my mother for this, especially once word of the beating spread through our extended family. My cousins teased me about it, threatening to tell my mother all sorts of made-up things to get me another beating.

Whenever a child in our family misbehaved, the adults would threaten them too, saying, "We'll send you to live with Lady Naa Lamiley so you can experience the Dorinda treatment." When children did poorly in school, the parents would say, "take a leaf out of Dorinda's book, she's smart. Remember, her mum says spare the rod and spoil the child." And I thought, if this is what it takes to be put on a pedestal, I'd rather just sit down on the floor, thank-you very much.

XOX ≡ X X ≡

Not every transgression was met with a beating, however. My mother was also quite good at teaching through the use of traditional stories. The following is one she told me after an episode less distressing than the red-light jaunt, but in which I had once again shown a serious lack of common sense. It happened one day when I was baby-sitting. My three younger siblings were driving me crazy, and I hit on an idea that might quiet them—reading aloud. No one could agree on a story, so I suggested that each choose their favorite book, and we'd read three stories.

We were then faced with the problem of how to get those favorite books down from where they resided, on the top shelf of the bookcase. I couldn't find a stepladder, and there were no high chairs in the sitting room where the bookcase stood.

Suddenly, I had a flash of inspiration—we would build our own stepladder! I sent Lynda out for a dining-room chair, which I flipped upside down and wedged, seat-first, into a bookshelf that happened to be the same height. This looked a little rickety, so I had Susan bring me a little traditional stool, which we placed over the upended chair legs. Almost there, but it needed to be more comfortable. I had little Sam bring me a pillow from the bedroom to top the whole thing off. I was very proud of my invention, but it still lacked some stability. So, before I sent Susan up for the books, I planted Lynda and Sam on each side of the "ladder," to hold it steady.

Well, that might have been fine if Susan, trying to keep her footing, hadn't dropped the books on the younger kids' heads. They jumped back, crying and screaming, and the whole thing came crashing down. When my mother rushed in, Susan's knee was bleeding and the rest of us were wailing. I expected a major thrashing, but instead my mother just sat me down and told me this story:

⁕⁕✕✕⁕⁕ ANANSE AND HIS WISDOM POT ⁕⁕✕✕⁕⁕

A long time ago, Kwaku Ananse the spider-man took a long, slow look at the rest of the world and said, "I don't like what I see. There are far too many people with brains and very, very few without brains. If I'm going to be able to trick people, I'll need to change this somehow. I must steal all the brains, wisdom, and intelligence from these clever people. Then everybody will be stupid except for me, and I'll be able to do anything I want."

So, Mr. Ananse made a huge ceramic pot with a tight lid and he went around the world stealing all the brains, cleverness, wisdom, and intelligence and stored it all in his big pot. After a few months, his mission was accomplished—he had hidden all the brains, cleverness, wisdom, and intelligence in his pot and all the people of the world had become stupid.

Mr. Ananse decided to hide his pot of brains at the top of the tallest tree he could find. To accomplish this, he made two strong leather belts to hold up the pot. One belt went around the pot then round his waist; the other one went around the pot and then over his shoulders. He looked pretty funny standing there, like he was hugely pregnant with other people's brains, cleverness, wisdom and intelligence, but he didn't care. After all, he had what he wanted. So, he started to shinny up the coconut tree. Up and up he climbed, inch by inch. It was slow and difficult because he needed all of his hands for climbing, making the pot even more unwieldy to maneuver.

All day Mr. Ananse tried to get his pot to the top of the tree, but by sunset he was only halfway up. He was tired and hungry. His thoughts began drifting home, where a pot of hot soup and fufu would surely be waiting for him. This is no use, he thought, I might as well give up.

Just then, he heard a child's voice at the bottom of the coconut tree. "Hey Mister," the voice said. "I could help you get your big pot to the top of the tree."

Mr. Ananse was in no mood for jokes. "Look kid, if this is your idea of a trick, forget it. And you'd better get out of here before I get my hands on you!"

But the kid persisted. "No sir, Mr. Ananse, you've got it all wrong. If you were to turn your pot around so that the belt parts came to the front and the pot sat on your back, you would find it a lot easier to climb this coconut tree."

Mr. Ananse considered what the child had said. He thought, The kid is surely right. But how can this little child have such cleverness when I have all the brains, intellect, and wisdom in my pot? Mr. Ananse thought some more, and suddenly the answer struck him. Common sense! He had forgotten to take the common sense when he was collecting all the rest of that stuff. "Oho," he crowed to himself, "I must go down and get it straight away."

Mr. Ananse was being greedy now. He was in such a hurry to grab this poor child's common sense that he did not take care coming down the tree. He slipped and fell to the ground and his ceramic pot broke into thousands of pieces, spreading the brains, intelligence, wisdom, and cleverness that he had so carefully collected. And that is how you and I got a piece of each.

Now, all we need to do is apply a bit of the common sense we've always had and we'll be right because, you see: *Book knowledge without common sense is useless.*

Then Mum took me by the hand and marched me back into the sitting room, calling for my brother and sisters to come watch. She turned the dining-room chair right-side up and told me to stand on the seat. I did. Then, handing me the fallen books, Mum said, ever so calmly, "Please put these on the shelf where they belong, Naa Tsenkua."

I took the books from her, reached up, and placed them on the top shelf.

Mum grinned broadly at us and said, "Now isn't that a whole lot easier?"

I Was Never Here
and This Never Happened

For the sake of this story I shall call her Mrs. Bonsu. She was my standard two (6th grade) teacher the year that Red and I had our adventure, and was like a mother to us. So, like any children, we hated her sometimes—more precisely, every weekday morning, when she insisted on inspecting the cleanliness of our nails, teeth, and underwear, as well as examining our hair for lice and nits. This seemed to be a stupid, futile routine—much like our weekly safety drills, emergency practices to be put in place should our school ever come under attack. We weren't happy when she gave us too many English composition pieces in any one week either, but we did love her much of the time as well. We especially loved her on Fridays when she not only taught us fun songs, but sang along with glee.

There's nothing to make you want to return to school on Monday like leaving for the weekend with a happy song still ringing in your ears. Mrs. Bonsu was clever that way, and I think she actually cared about us. She had been the resident standard two teacher for a few years by the time I entered her class, and we studied almost all of our subjects with her.

This was the mid 1950s at Yaa Achia Girls School in Kumasi.

Those were innocent carefree times for us kids, but much less so for the adults around us. In fact, they were turbulent times of political unrest, arrests, betrayals, factions, and armed conflicts between the ruling party members and their opposition counterparts. This included unmitigated violent attacks, not only on public figures or political activists, but on seemingly innocent bystanders as well. Needless to say, our parents were very concerned about our safety, particularly on our way to and from school each day, as this often entailed walking several miles through districts loyal to differing political factions.

Some parents got together and formed car pools to take their kids to and from school while others, like my mother, paid trusted taxi drivers to do it. I was taken to and from school every day by Papa Asamoah, our family's regular taxi driver. If we were more than thirty minutes late getting home, my mother would be worried, pacing the floor and dispatching other friendly taxi drivers to search for us. That was the frenetic backdrop of the time and many of us kids were affected by it.

On the day in question, Mrs. Bonsu surprised us. We only ever sang on Fridays, but this once she broke with tradition and started teaching us a song in the middle of the week. This incongruity intrigued the entire class, and we watched intently as she wrote the song's words in white chalk on the blackboard, humming the tune as she wrote. The song began:

Osei Bonsu, Opoku Fofie, Osei Yaw, Osei Yaw Akoto,
Kwaku Duah Odikan, Kofi Karikari, Mensah Bonsu,
Kwaku Duah, Prempeh.

At last it became clear—this wasn't a singing lesson at all, it was just a very unusual history teaching technique. For the above are not song lyrics at all; it's a chronological list of names of Ashanti chiefs preceding the incumbent reigning monarch at the time.

Mrs. Bonsu turned to face the class and launched into full singing voice as she proudly enunciated each chief's name with a little sideways roll of her head and a rhythmic stamp of her foot. She sang the whole history through once and then launched into a second rendition. She did not finish. Mid song, a huge brown egg came flying through the classroom window and landed under her desk. Her voice changed from melodious to a panicked shrill as she called out to us: "A grenade, quick children, hide!"

Suddenly our hated weekly emergency routine didn't seem so pointless. We moved fast and efficiently, like a well trained military unit, straight into position as practiced. We overturned our little wooden desks to form a barrier, then crouched, grouped together in a tight bunch behind the shielding cordon. That was when it happened—a big BANG, a massive explosion followed by dead silence. It all happened so fast yet in slow motion. The classroom was filled with thick smoke and the smell of burning flesh.

At first no one moved, then one child screamed that another child had wet herself. Other kids started to jump up calling out "kai" ("yuck") even though the wetness was nowhere near them; as they did so, others pushed their immediate neighbors away claiming that they were treading on their toes or pulling on their school uniforms. In a few seconds we had turned on each other like a pack of wolves, jostling and yapping at each other in our terror. No one noticed Mrs. Bonsu at first.

Suddenly, one of the pushing, jostling, squabbling children stopped cold and pointed, staring with her mouth wide open, unable to make a sound. Slowly we all stopped and turned to follow her gaze. The blackboard and desk were covered with blood and body parts, the remains of our beloved teacher. Twenty-eight children froze in place, as though hypnotized.

Other teachers had heard the explosion and came rushing in to find a most macabre spectacle—Mrs. Bonsu blown to smithereens by a hand grenade, her pupils standing huddled together blankly staring.

I do not remember much about what happened next or how we got out of there but I do remember our next classroom. We had no desk or chairs, just some grass under the mango trees, where we usually went for art class. We sat in a semicircle around our new teacher, who was younger and less motherly than Mrs. Bonsu and, instead of regular classwork, she told us traditional stories for the rest of the school year.

Nobody ever discussed that fateful day with us. There was no counseling, no child psychologist to take us through the grieving process. Nobody, child or adult, brought up the subject again. It was as if we had signed a collective oath of secrecy, as if to talk about it was bad luck, a taboo that would make it all happen again. We were afraid to raise the dead, so to speak, and so we were each left with our memories and our pain. We learned to bury it deep in the recesses of our souls, as children do with any other deep trauma.

A number of my school friends did wet themselves more often in class, others stuttered for a long time afterwards. And I began having trouble making sense out of things written in white chalk on blackboards—when written in any other color it was fine. Well into my high school years, I still had trouble stopping my hand trembling whenever I had to take notes on cultural history. That I think may also explain why I have had such trouble, such insomnia, such panic attacks recalling the incidence of that day. In retrospect, the element of doubt and denial has now set in and some people who were there even claim the incident never occurred. That is part of my nightmare and also why I often ask myself whether I was ever there and whether those things actually happened.

To this day, I have never properly learned the full names and correct succession order of our Ashanti chiefs.

Here is one of the stories that we learned as part of those therapeutic tale-telling sessions under the mango trees.

APPOINTMENT WITH DEATH

In the old, old days long ago, human beings never died. When they got tired of living their lives, they just changed into whatever animal they fancied, and lived a different sort of life. After a few score years, when they got tired of that, they could become another sort of animal, or a tree, or the wind. Then, after a few more years, they could change back to being human. In fact, even though everything is different now, that's why we still talk to the wind and to animals, because even today they carry the spirits of those early people. But that's not what this story is about.

So back then all the beings lived happily together—all the beings except Death, that is. He had once been human, but had been banished for his nasty, unpleasant personality and antisocial behavior. He lived alone in a cave in a faraway land, but even though he was an outcast, he missed human company. He was always asking people in various different cities and towns and villages if he could come and visit them, but nobody trusted him—they knew that every time Death came around, bad things seemed to happen. Still, it was a real obsession with him, and he just kept asking.

This particular week, Death asked to come and visit our part of the world. Indeed, he was waiting at the entrance to the big city of Kumasi. The town elders decided that three brave, strong, young people should be found to go tell him that he was not welcome. Just like in the times of the tribal wars, young people were always being encouraged to do chivalrous things for their tribe, and even for their country, but this was something different. This time the danger was so high that the chief decided to offer three million pounds as an incentive to volunteers. So, the news went out by town crier to all the people of Kumasi: the chief needs three brave, strong, athletic youngsters, and he's willing to pay very well for the job. Eventually, three brave young school friends volunteered and were accepted. After a briefing from the chief's advisers on how exactly to let Death know that he wasn't wanted, they set off for the edge of town.

There were no cars back then, so they had to walk. And there wasn't much to look at on the way—once word of Death's visit got out, shopkeepers bolted their doors and windows, parents kept their children inside, and the streets were generally deserted. This made the long journey seem even longer, and to keep their spirits up the three friends laughed and joked, teasing and jostling each other.

But halfway to the meeting place, the three friends realized that they had been foolish. In their excitement about saving the city from Death's visit, they had forgotten to bring any food or drinks, and there was still quite a ways to go. Tired, hungry, and thirsty, they hit upon a solution. They would draw straws, and the one who drew the shortest straw would have to walk all the way back until he found somewhere to get some refreshments while the other two took a well-deserved rest in the shade. They all agreed, and lots were drawn.

But no sooner had the loser set off for the center of town, than one of the remaining friends turned to his companion and said, "Hey, are you thinking what I'm thinking?"

"I don't know what you're thinking," his friend replied, "but what I'm thinking is pretty wild." So they shared their thoughts, and what do you know? They were both thinking the same greedy, wicked thought. That is, that if some nasty accident should happen to befall the third friend, and he never returned, they would be able to split his share of the reward money.

"After all," the first one pointed out, "why share three million pounds between three people when we can share it between two instead?" They sat there for a little while, imagining what might happen to their friend, and what each would do with all that money. Finally, one of them jumped up and blurted out, "Let's just kill him when he returns. Nobody will ever know—we can say that Death made off with him." So they shook hands on the deal, a complicated secret handshake that they made up on the spot. And then they lay down to take a nap, preparing to pounce on their friend as soon as he arrived.

Now the third friend, he who had drawn the short straw, was not very happy at that moment. Why, he asked himself as he trudged back to town, did he always have to do the lousy jobs? Did his two friends ever pick the short straw? No, they didn't. They must be in it together, always plotting behind his back. The longer he walked in the heat, the sun beating down on his head, the more paranoid he became, and by the time he finally got back into town, he had hatched his own evil plan. He would show his friends, he thought. He'd teach *them* to gang up on him. He decided to buy the food and drinks, as planned, but to eat his portion first and then poison the remainder. He'd take that to his friends and watch them die. Then he'd finish the errand on his own, and return to sorrowfully announce that Death had stolen his two friends—and, of course, claim all of the money for himself.

And so he managed to find the only shop open in town (its proprietors were both stone deaf, and hadn't heard the town crier's warnings that Death was coming), bought the food, ate his fill, and then poisoned the rest as planned. But when he returned to his famished friends, they set upon him as though they were possessed and beat him to death with sticks and stones. Then, content to have carried out their evil plan, they shook hands again (using, of course, their secret complicated handshake) and sat down to enjoy the meal brought to them by their now-dead friend. But the food he had brought them was poisoned, so they too fell dead.

And so it was that the three school friends all kept their appointment with Death, although not in the way anyone had imagined. And as for Death himself, when no one showed up to turn him away, he assumed that he was at last welcome back among human beings, and so he entered the town at last and stayed forever.

Do As I Say or I'll Pepper You

All my young life I had heard certain grown-ups (although certainly not my parents or other family members) tell their children, "Do as I say or I'll pepper you." I had never really known what that meant, taking it as some random turn of phrase, a grown-up joke, an empty threat. Not until I went away to my first boarding school did I learn differently.

That school was Mmofraturo Methodist Girls Boarding School, and every year they handed out application forms to various local schools in Kumasi, to encourage them to recommend potential new entrants. I was lucky to have been one of only five students at my school to be put forward, but my mother said I couldn't go. I begged her to discuss it with Dad.

Dad agreed with Mum that we couldn't afford it, but he was willing to send me anyway. Mum said I was too young. Dad reminded Mum that I was ten now and that I'd been baby-sitting my two younger siblings very capably for the last four years. Mum said I would miss home. Dad countered that I needed to spend more time with my peers; he said since I'd put in the extra effort to qualify for Mmofraturo and succeeded, I should be rewarded for my achievement.

Dorinda, age 12, at Mmofraturo Girls boarding school

It was settled. I could scarcely wait to pack the "medium metal trunk" full of labelled clothes that all new students were supposed to bring, along with the wooden "chop-box" of provisions that were also required. To wit,

6 tins of corned beef
6 tins of sardines
6 tins of baked beans
6 cans of evaporated milk
1 big jar of chile sambal (homemade)
1 bottle of tomato ketchup
1 big bag of gari (coarse cassava powder)
1 packet of salt
2 tins of margarine
1 big, round tin of processed cheese
6 cakes of bath soap
1 tube of toothpaste
6 rolls of toilet paper

and in the trunk:

6 pairs of white socks
6 pairs of underwear
6 handkerchiefs
3 bed sheets
3 pillow cases
3 night dresses
2 bath towels
2 cakes of laundry soap
2 pairs of achimota sandals
1 cotton draw-string toilet bag
1 tooth brush
1 flashlight with batteries

Aunty Betty and Aunty Sophie made sure I had everything on the list. I could always count on my Aunty Sophie to come through for me. She wasn't really a blood relative, but our closest family friend who just happened to live across the road from us, and she was like a twin sister to my mum. They dressed very similarly (they'd often buy the same fabrics), they wore their hair the same (they shared a hairdresser and jeweler), they shared a love of cooking and often swapped recipes—and their husbands were even born on the same day! Mum and Aunty Sophie saw each other's children as their own, and they treated all equally. We in turn loved them both.

Ah, no more baby-sitting my siblings (except on my visits home), no more cleaning my mother's room (except on school holidays), no more being treated like a child. Finally, I was on my way to my first independent adventure, a sleepover with girlfriends that would last three months at a time. I was beside myself with anticipation.

Mmofraturo Methodist Girls Boarding School was set on sweeping, stunningly landscaped grounds, nestled comfortably between baobab and palm trees and flowering jacarandas. The word "mmofra" means children and "turo" means garden, so the name of the school literally meant "children's garden." In keeping with this theme, our school uniforms came in a wide range of pastel colors. The first time I stepped onto campus and saw a veritable garden of potential friends dressed like spring flowers in uniforms of lavender, pink, yellow, mint green, blue, and soft pale orange, I knew I was in a special paradise reserved just for girls.

Never mind that for the first time in my life I had to use communal latrines or that the food tasted like boiled cardboard. I had my tins of corned beef and I was on my own. I could spend as much time as I liked with my friends and I savored every moment, worried that my first three months here might pass by too quickly.

Each group of sixteen girls shared one house, which was divided into three dormitories, four to six girls per dorm. Our dormitory was in House Four. At night, all of the girls in House Four would sneak out of beds and cram together into one room, where we'd stay up late and chat. Most of us in my dormitory were first-year students, and we found our new freedom exhilarating.

Lights out was at eight o'clock during the school week, and nine on weekends. After the teacher turned out the lights, we were expected to stop gossiping and yapping and go to sleep, but of course, girls will be girls; we liked to play and carry on, especially if there was a particularly juicy story we wanted to hear. That first week we managed to keep it somewhat under control for the first five nights, but on our first Saturday together we broke loose, talking and laughing well into the night. It was about half past one in the morning when one of the teachers finally came around to check on us for the third time.

Selina was in the middle of telling us how her parents had caught her big brother sneaking girls into their house at night, when our math teacher, Miss Adomako, suddenly appeared in the doorway.

"Young ladies," she said stiffly, "come with me."

Still in our nighties, we marched outside as ordered. The gravel crunched under our bare feet and the stars overhead flickered indifferently. We followed her into the teacher's house, all the way up the stairs to the very top landing. There we were lined up facing Mrs. Duah, the head teacher, who walked back and forth in front of us, lecturing us on the necessity of obedience to school rules. Miss Adomako handed her a little bowl, which contained a thick ball of paste; the paste was a reddish-brown color, with stringy light brown fibers running through it. Mrs. Duah took a little pinch off the ball, rolled it between her fingers and, placing it on a teaspoon, handed it to Hope Asiedu, the first girl in the line. Mrs. Duah made more balls from the paste and she handed us each one on the end of the teaspoonful. Then much to my horror, she told us all to spread our legs.

Her face completely impassive, Mrs. Duah instructed Hope to put the little ball of paste up into her vagina. "Now, cross your legs, Hope."

At the time I wasn't sure what was in that ball of paste, but judging from the way Hope was jumping around and crying, I was suspicious that whatever it contained was burning her terribly.

Mrs. Duah then told Angelina Sackey, the second girl in line, to do the same. Upon insertion, the poor girl displayed the same behavior as Hope, hopping up and down with her legs crossed, crying in pain.

I suppose the idea was that once you'd been peppered you would never, never misbehave again. But I was fourth in line and seeing what happened to the first three, I thought *bugger this*. So, when it was my turn, I shoved my hand a little further up my nightie and deposited the ball of paste into my belly button. Acting as though I was modest, I managed to cover the procedure with my other hand, so Miss Duah, who was standing over me watching, didn't cotton onto my deception. And then I crossed my legs and started jumping. I was the biggest drama queen you have ever seen. I hopped and grimaced and groaned, just like all the others were doing, being sure to keep my hand over my belly button so the ball of paste didn't fall out.

Of course, after we had been there for an hour being lectured my belly button was in absolute agony, but nothing like what the other girls were suffering. The next day, one of the older students told me exactly what had been in that paste: a mixture of ground chile peppers, a little bit of gingerroot, some peppercorns, and just enough water to make a thick paste.

Well, I wasted no time in writing a letter to my mother about this atrocious punishment and, as I expected, she was at the school in a flash. I begged her to let me come back home—that last experience had changed my opinion of my heavenly boarding school—but she went one better. She got my Uncle Comey, who was Justice Mills-Odoi, a legal advisor to the government, to write a letter to the school's headmistress strongly deploring the barbaric practice of using chile to discipline girls, and further threatened legal action, the shutdown of the school, and all sorts of other things if Mmofraturo did not immediately cease and desist this activity.

I am pleased to say that this form of punishment was hastily withdrawn, and my association with the "children's garden" continued for quite some time without further trauma.

XOX ⠿ X X ⠿

When I visited home from boarding school, I was always happy to eat at my Aunty Sophie's. One of her favorite meals, chicken with gravy, mashed yams, and rice, was real down-home comfort-food, ideal for cheering up any boarding-school girls whose corn-beef stock was running low.

I WAS NEVER HERE...

✕✕ **SEASONED CHICKEN** ✕✕

SERVES 4-6

12 chicken wings
1 clove garlic, finely chopped
2 tablespoons ground cumin
$^1/_2$ cup (4 fl oz/125 ml) corn oil
$^1/_2$ cup (4 fl oz/125 ml) water
1 tablespoon paprika powder
4 teaspoons garlic salt
Juice of 1 lemon
1 tablespoon finely chopped thyme
1 tablespoon finely chopped parsley
1 tablespoon finely chopped basil

Prepare the chicken by removing the wing tips and cutting each wing into two halves (a drumette and a flat bit), so that you have 24 pieces of chicken altogether.

Mix together all the remaining ingredients, pour over the chicken pieces, mixing to coat all pieces very well.

Cover and marinate overnight in the refrigerator.

The next day, arrange the chicken pieces in a baking dish, pour the marinade juices over them, and bake in a hot oven for 20 minutes.

Lower the heat to medium low and drain off the juices, reserving them to add to the rice once it's boiling.

Return the chicken to the oven and continue cooking until the pieces are cooked through and evenly browned. Serve hot with rice, gravy, and mashed yam croquettes (see recipe page 107).

✕✕ **GRAVY** ✕✕

$^1/_2$ cup (4 fl oz/125 ml) corn oil

3 medium onions, peeled and finely chopped

2 large red chile peppers, seeded and finely
   chopped

2 teaspoons tomato paste

1 cup (8 fl oz/250 ml) cold water

4 large ripe tomatoes, blanched in hot water,
   peeled and diced

Salt to taste

Black pepper to taste

In a large skillet, heat the corn oil and fry the onions until lightly browned.

Add the chiles and cook for one more minute.

Dissolve the tomato paste in the water, then add it and the tomatoes to the fried onions and stir well. Salt and pepper to taste.

Simmer slowly on low heat until slightly reduced, approximately another 10–15 minutes.

I WAS NEVER HERE...

✖✖ MASHED YAM CROQUETTES ✖✖

2 cups (1 lb/500 g) boiled and smoothly mashed
  yams or sweet potatoes, or one cup of each
1 cup (8 oz/250 g) fresh bread crumbs
¹/₄ cup (2 oz/60 g) butter, melted
2 teaspoons ground white pepper
1 tablespoon each very finely diced red and green
  bell pepper
3 large eggs
Salt to taste
1 cup (8 oz/250 g) cornstarch
2 cups (16 fl oz/500 ml) vegetable oil, for frying
Lettuce leaves, for serving

In a large mixing bowl, combine the mashed yams and/or sweet potatoes, bread crumbs, melted butter, white pepper, the bell pepper, one of the eggs, and a dash of salt. Mix together thoroughly and form into small-ish (one-to-two inch-long) sausage-shaped croquettes, about an inch in diameter, or ping-pong-ball-sized spheres.

Beat the other two eggs in a separate bowl, and season to taste with salt. Dip each of the croquettes first in beaten egg and then in cornstarch, to coat. Heat the vegetable oil until it starts to smoke slightly, and fry the croquettes a few at a time until they are quite brown all over. Remove from oil and drain on paper towels. Keep warm on a plate in the oven until ready to serve.

Serve on leaves of lettuce with the chicken, rice, and gravy.

The Fire That Melted the Butter
Must Have Coddled the Eggs

Even though Mmofraturo was only seven or eight miles away from my mum's work, school policy discouraged visits home outside of the standard holidays. Thus these visits home seemed especially precious—although I wouldn't exactly call them vacations, certainly not by comparison to how my school chums spent their holidays. Mine were full of mothers giving birth to babies left, right, and center—on the doorstep, in taxis, in the market outside— normal births, difficult births, births inside our front door and, only occasionally, on the maternity beds where they were *meant* to be taking place. My mum and Aunty Thelma had created a sensation among the competitive practitioners of midwifery with the introduction of the prenatal clinics, and it was known throughout the surrounding countryside that you really should have your baby at Thelma's. So, pregnant mothers and babies seemed to materialize everywhere, and never at a convenient time.

Things were still quite unsettled politically, and it's probably just as well that I was attending boarding school, because many kids my age had gotten involved with a militant young people's movement known as the young pioneers. This formidable organization recruited its members from people between the ages of five and twenty-five. Local branches were in contact with a national head office, linked directly to the Convention People's Party, one of the parties vying for control of Ghana. Regular weekly meetings were held in every district, and members were expected to act as the ruling party's "eyes." The young pioneers were indoctrinated with nationalistic slogans and catchy songs. They wore beautifully tailored uniforms and conducted well-drilled marches on state and important political occasions and public holidays.

In those days of virtually indiscriminate political imprisonments, it was not at all unusual for arrest and conviction to be based on the testimony of a young pioneer, who might well be the accused party's son or daughter. As we've seen in so many similar situations, those impetuous youngsters were easily indoctrinated, and would consider it their civic duty to report to their leaders any comments that they felt were in any way critical or derogatory of "the party." I say "impetuous" because these kids were egged on by their leaders, and often the full consequence of their actions wouldn't hit home until a paddy wagon, or a "go inside" as they were colloquially known, arrived to take Mummy or Daddy away to an unknown destination. Too late, they would realize that there was no way of knowing when Mummy or Daddy would return, if ever, and now there was only the extended family to rely on to help with homework or provide food and shelter.

Some of my local chums belonged to the young pioneers, and I wished that I too could have joined but, because of attending Mmofraturo, I was gone for months at a time, and thus not a candidate. Of course I had no idea what all of the political ramifications of being a young pioneer were, I just loved the sound of their rhythmic recitations, affirmations and songs. But most of all, I was envious of their beautiful gray/blue uniforms, with their eye-catching little red neckerchiefs. Often I longed to trade in my pastel boarding-school uniform for one—until I was rudely awakened to the true nature of all this political intriguing.

The incident in question took place on one of my rare vacations on which, of course, I was helping out at Thelma's. It was not unusual for women in labor to thump on our huge, wooden front doors in the middle of the night, seeking urgent assistance to deliver their babies. Indeed my mother could rarely leave—all three of my siblings and I were born and grew up on the premises. Aunt Thelma and Mum never seemed to get much caught up in the rampant political turmoil outside their doors—they didn't have the time. Ghanaian women seem to like having babies, and every single one of them seemed to me to be having hers at Thelma's. It got so crazy that these two midwives at one point had to hire nannies to take care of their own children!

So, all this is by way of saying that we weren't the least bit surprised one night when we heard the hammering on our front door at 2 AM, and a major commotion outside. This sort of thing was quite ordinary, but even so, somehow this particular knocking was unusually urgent. Could it be an impatient frightened husband?

We had some seven babies in cots next to their mothers' beds, including a set of twin boys, and I was dedicating my school holiday to helping out wherever I could. Still, Mum hadn't had the time to sleep or eat in nearly twenty-four hours. She had been with the mother of the twins throughout her labor; fetching her drinks, washing her down, mopping her brow, examining her and reassuring her all the way.

In fact, Mum had only just climbed into the big wooden bed she shared with my two younger sisters, who were one and three years old, when the knocking started. Mum whispered to me, and I sat up in my little single bed, which stood in an alcove off of Mum's bedroom.

Mum called out as clearly as she could without waking the sleeping patients, "Hold on, we're coming."

I could hear her shuffling slowly out of bed and muttering under her breath as she did so, then pulling her robe from where she'd slung it over the dividers separating my little cubicle from her room. But before she could even put it on, the front door was literally flung off its hinges by a blow from a sledgehammer. This was a first, even for a nervous father!

Then three tall men, their faces hidden behind cloth masks, burst into our bedroom. Only their eyes were showing. For one fleeting moment, I thought I might still be dreaming, because this was so much like the westerns I used to watch at the local cinema. Clearly these were the bad guys, and any minute now Roy Rogers or Doris Day would appear to rescue me. But these were no lonesome cowboys. They wore khaki shorts, loud purple and green patterned cotton shirts, baseball caps, and dark glasses. Yes, dark glasses at two in the morning, and they smelt of stale sweat and something else I did not recognize. A frightening picture under any circumstances, but especially these. I was out of bed like a flash and hanging onto my mum for dear life.

The biggest of the men spoke first. He demanded to know where my dad was. Although I was too young to understand at the time, I'm sure he was trying to ascertain his political allegiances, and possibly grill him on whatever the burning issues of the time were. But my parents led such separate lives most of the time, Mum probably couldn't have answered even if she'd wanted to. And of course she didn't.

And indeed, Mum said she didn't know. The ringleader repeated the question several times, and each time her answer was the same. Finally, frustrated with this uncooperative woman, he hit my mum hard with something (I couldn't catch exactly what) he'd been holding in his hand. She lost her balance and fell against the bed.

The man looked around the room and for the first time noticed me. He leaned forward and pulled me towards his face. He had a big face and I felt like I was looking into the eyes of a giant puppet except this one smelt bad and hit people. I hated him instantly.

The voice from behind his mask roared at me, "Where is your father?"

I was very frightened. I could hear my heart beating inside my chest, but I managed to croak out, "Mum's told you, he is not here."

"Where is he?" he bellowed, shaking me with his strong, callused hands.

I squeaked back what I thought was a really loud reply, "I don't know."

The man lifted up what he was holding in his other hand and I thought he was going to hit me too, like he did my mum. I ducked instinctively but he pulled me up by my nightie and slowly pointed what I now realized was a gun at my face. As my legs flailed helplessly in the air I wished that my growth spurt had hit early; I was small for my age to begin with.

The man held me up like a rag doll and without taking his eyes off me, he spoke to my mum, "Since you can't remember where your own husband is, perhaps you can remember where you are hiding Mr. Sarpong's twins. We hear the wife came in here to deliver his little mongrels; you deliver them to me and I'll spare your little girl." And with that, he levelled the double-barreled gun right at my eyes.

All I could think was that the two metal tubes looked just like a man's nostrils. It was all I could do to keep from remarking on this, but giddy as I was, I knew that I was in mortal danger. I glanced up at Mum for reassurance and realized for the first time that she had blood all over her face. Starting to shake, I felt as though I would wet my pants. No one spoke for a few seconds as I stared into those black nostrils.

Slowly, the man let go of me and lifted the gun to my mum's head. By this time he was impatient and wild, his eyes flashing as he bellowed, "Speak, woman!"

I thought he was going to kill my mum. I rushed to hold onto her, totally panicked. As I hunched over, shaking uncontrollably, my arms wrapped around her, I felt the urine running down my legs. I lifted my head to see if anyone was watching. And when I did, I came face to face with the largest set of balls I had ever seen, clearly outlined against the man's thin khaki shorts.

I figured they were going to kill us all, we had nothing to lose, and so quick as a flash I leaned forward, opened my mouth wide, and bit those balls as hard as I could. The wooden butt of the gun came crashing down on my head and I collapsed to the floor, blood flowing freely from my scalp.

As the man shrieked with pain, shaking his head violently from side to side, his cloth mask slipped down.

Through my pain, I heard my mother's voice, now strong and fearless, "Osei Sibeh, I gave life to your premature baby and now you thank me by killing my daughter and me! For hours I sat by your baby's bed, not daring to sleep in case he stopped breathing. I collected breast milk from other nursing mothers to feed him with an eyedropper. And now this?"

There was an uneasy silence in which I fully expected to hear the gunfire begin. Instead, a miracle occurred. Slowly, slowly, the man I had bitten pulled the cloth mask from around his neck where it had come to rest. There stood a bearded, good-looking young black man with nostrils just like gun barrels. He sank to the floor at my mum's feet and started crying and apologizing, "You're safe mama...your babies...the baby twins are safe mama...they'll all be safe, mama...."

My mum did not move. I did not move. The other two men did not move. We stayed, frozen in time and thought. After what seemed like an interminable period, Osei Sibeh spoke again. He stood up and ordered his own men out of our house, threatening to kill them and anybody else who dared to come near us again.

From that day onwards, we had protection; the word was out on the streets that Thelma's Maternity Home was sacred property. And that is how it was that I never heard again the thwack! thwack! of the machete outside our bedroom window as it was brought down on someone running to seek a safe haven in the maternity home, nor the screams for help before the thud! thud! of the big-headed walking sticks landed on the skull of some poor hapless soul in the night and everything went still again. That was why my mum no longer had to send people to wash blood from outside our windows in the mornings.

As an adult, I look back on the mixture of joy and horror that was my childhood in Ghana, and marvel that I never became schizophrenic, or worse. I suppose the old cooking expression has some truth here—the same fire that melts the butter also coddles the eggs.

There is deadly turmoil in many traditional stories too, but usually it's solved by cleverness, not force, as in this story about the ever-resourceful Mr. Ananse.

THE FANTASTIC LYING CONTEST

One day, the fly, the ant, and the mosquito went hunting together. They came upon Mr. Ananse, the spider, in the forest, and decided to gang up on him. But Ananse was stronger than he looked and, after a mighty struggle, they had to stop for a rest.

"Why are you trying to kill me?" Ananse asked them.

"Because we are hungry," they replied. "After all, everybody needs to eat."

"Well, I need to eat too," he said. "Why shouldn't I eat you?"

"You aren't strong enough to overpower us," they answered, in one voice.

"Ah, but nor are you three strong enough to overpower me," he pointed out. "So let's make a bargain. Each of us will tell the others a most extraordinarily fantastic story. If I say I don't believe any of your three stories, you may eat me. And if you don't believe my story, I will eat you."

This sounded fair enough. The ant went first. "Before I was born," said the ant, "my father inherited a new piece of land. But the very first day he went out to clear it, he cut his foot with a bush knife and couldn't work it. So I jumped out of my mother's womb, cleared the land, cultivated the ground, planted it, harvested my crop, and sold it at the market. When I was born a few days later, my father was already a rich man."

The three friends looked at Ananse expectantly, waiting for him to call this a lie so they could eat him. But instead he said, "Ah, how interesting. Clearly this story has a ring of truth about it."

Then the mosquito told his story. "One day when I was only four years old," he began, "I was sitting in the forest, peacefully gnawing on an elephant I had killed, when a leopard crept up on me. He opened his jaws to swallow me, but I just reached my hand down his throat, grabbed the inside of his tail, and gave it a good yank to turn him inside out. Well, it seems this leopard had just eaten a sheep, because suddenly the sheep was on the outside and the leopard inside *him*. The sheep thanked me quite profusely, and went off to graze somewhere else."

Again, the hunting partners waited for Ananse to denounce this story as a lie, because they were quite eager to make a meal of him, but instead he said, "What a fascinating story. How I love to hear fantastic things!"

So then the fly took his turn. "Just the other day," he said, "I came upon an antelope. I aimed my gun at him and fired, then ran up and caught him, threw him to the ground, skinned him, and dressed the meat. Just then the bullet from my gun came along, so I caught it and put it back in my pocket. I carried the antelope meat up into the tallest tree around, built a fire, cooked up the entire antelope, and ate it all. But when it was time to climb down, I had eaten so much and my stomach was so swollen that I was too heavy to climb. So I went back to the village and got a rope, which I brought back to the tree I was in. Then I tied the rope around my waist and carefully let myself down to the ground."

The three waited patiently for Ananse to say, "You are lying," but instead he cried, "Ah, what a miraculous true story!"

Finally, it was Ananse's turn to tell a tale. "Last year," he said, "I planted a coconut tree. One month later, it had grown very tall, and was bearing fruit. I was hungry, so I harvested three ripe coconuts. When I opened the first one, a fly flew out. I opened the second, and an ant crawled out. And when I opened the third one, out flew a mosquito. Now clearly, since I had planted the coconut tree, the ant, the fly, and the mosquito belonged to me. But when I tried to eat them, they ran away. I have been searching for them ever since so that I could eat them, as it's only fair—and now, at last I've found you."

The three hunters were silent. If they said, as Ananse had to their stories "How true, how true," then he would be within his rights to claim them as his property, and he would eat them. But if they said that he had lied, then by the rules of the contest he would also be allowed to eat them. They couldn't make up their minds what to say, so they turned tail and ran away as fast as they could.

And ever since then, Ananse has eaten every mosquito, fly, and ant he catches, because he outwitted them in the lying contest.

The Way to the River

"Give a man a fish and he'll eat it once, show him the way to the river and you've fed him for life."

—EMMA AFARCHOE OKINE
(MY GRANDMA)

After my stint at Mmofraturo, I was accepted into another prestigious boarding school, Wesley Girls High School— a private, all-girls secondary boarding school, rather like present-day Methodist Ladies' Colleges elsewhere. Started in September, 1836 by Mrs. Harriet Wrigley, the wife of a Methodist missionary, Wesley's original aim was "to give the girls basic education with emphasis on domestic science, to prepare the young women for marriage to the elite gentry." But, after passing through the hands of a series of strong, capable early pioneering women, the present school came into its own in 1884. Goodness knows but Mrs. Harriet Wrigley would turn in her grave if she realized that Wesley Girls has produced some of the most high-powered independent professional women in the country, including, to name a few, Africa's first woman pilot, the Assistant Director General of the International Labor Organization in the United Nations, Ghana's first female broadcast engineer, and so on.

The school now prides itself on giving its students an all-round education; with academic excellence, discipline, self-respect, grooming, and decorum high on the list, and a healthy dose of religion thrown in for good measure. At the time I was there the majority of our students were black Africans, although from a wide range of backgrounds: there were kids whose parents were rich businessmen and women—or just rich, such as daughters of public figures, professionals, and politicians. And then there were the poor village kids who just happened to be bright enough to secure one of the few coveted full or half scholarships awarded nationally each year for academic excellence.

When I arrived at Wey Gey Hey, as it was affectionately called, I still had many ghosts I needed to lay to rest. One ongoing source of distress was my looks—I had decided around the age of twelve that if beauty was wealth, then I could safely be classified as poor, very poor. This was confirmed for me by various different relatives, neighbors and friends. When they came to visit my mother, they would point to my long-limbed, fair-skinned younger sister Susan and say, "What a pretty girl, she looks just like one of those European dolls." Then upon sighting the next youngest sister, Lynda, who was much darker, they'd continue, "Oh, she's a black beauty, just like one of our own dolls. A true black olive." Lastly, they'd spot my brother Sam, the youngest of us all, and comment, "See how manly and strong he looks? One day he'll turn into a strapping beefcake!"

Just as they were heading out the door, my mother would exclaim, "But what about Dorinda, did you not see her?" More in response to the exasperation in her voice than anything else, the culprit would reply without so much as a backward glance:

"OOOh, she's got character!"

And then they'd hurry away before anyone could stop them for an explanation. I got used to this.

Lynda, Dorinda, and Susan, with Sam in front, after Sunday service in Kumasi

AND THIS NEVER HAPPENED

That was one of the reasons that I was so elated when I scored a full scholarship to Wesley Girls High School. This, I promised myself, was going to be the unveiling of Charity Dorinda. I would make my mark one way or another. And in many ways, this did happen—both physically (more on that in a bit) and more importantly, mentally, I stopped being a child while at Wey Gey Hey.

XXX ᴵᴵᴵᴵᴵ X X ᴵᴵᴵᴵᴵ

Based on the principle that those more fortunate should give back to the community, Wesley Girls High School initiated a program wherein the senior girls were allowed to do pastoral work in the adjoining village of Kakumdo. On Sunday mornings, a select group of six or eight girls would be dispatched to the tiny village, about a mile from the school. Half of the group would administer first aid, as part of our Red Cross training. The other half, known as the Preaching Group, would conduct church services; they read parables from the bible, and recited Christian songs and hymns for groups of both adults and children.

The Preaching and First Aid Groups swapped roles on alternate weeks. I particularly liked being in the First Aid Group, considering it a necessary prerequisite for my intended career in nursing. In order to qualify for the group, I had to first pass my Red Cross exam and be a paid-up holder of a Red Cross certificate and badge, which I wore with pride. Our services to the village ranged from disinfecting wounds with Dettol, iodine and other antiseptics, applying Band-Aids, plaster, or lint and a bandage, to extracting superficial thorns and foreign bodies from hands and feet.

I remember feeling honored and responsible in our roles as workers, and at the same time supercilious and arrogant, because we Wesley girls were educated.

One seemingly ordinary Sunday I was struck with a sense of foreboding that I just could not shake off. I was up unusually early that day, showered, dressed, and ready before any of the others were even out of bed. For some strange reason, I felt I had to be prepared should anything happen, but what? I told this to my colleagues when we set off for Kakumdo that morning and they teased me, saying, "Prophet Charity is about to see into the future." We all had a laugh at my expense, and I tried to think no more about it.

When we reached the village, we set up our little dispensary as usual on a small wooden table underneath a shade tree just off the central square. The Preaching Group had gathered a few children into a semicircle and were beginning their sermon. A few adults lay stretched out around the square, relaxing on the mats casually strewn under various trees. Several small groups of elders sat in clusters chatting in the shade. Everybody was in a lazy mood, except the big goat tethered to a central tree post in the middle of the village square and a few chickens running about. The goat was busily chewing on what tiny new shoots the poor tree was trying to grow. Even though it was early morning, the day had all the makings of a tropical scorcher; up above, the sky was a clear and striking blue.

I had only just attacked my second wound with an iodine swab when we heard a distinct humming coming from the sky. People craned their necks and swirled around, searching for the source of the noise. The hum got louder and nearer until it was downright deafening.

Suddenly the village was abuzz with activity, even pandemonium, as elders shepherded young kids inside the huts, beckoning us to follow them into the protection of their weather-beaten homes. Naked people with half-lathered heads and bodies rushed blindly from the washing alcoves, soap and water still running down their backs and into their faces. They gathered their infants and toddlers along the way. People were yelling out instructions to run for shelter, some were grabbing up mats and stools as others aided the old and infirm. Stubborn children received a slap around the ears as they were dragged, protesting, to safety.

Although we were only sixteen years old, our perceived status made us feel responsible towards the villagers, and we refused to abandon the village square until we were convinced there were no children left outside. The noise continued to get louder and closer, until finally we could make out exactly where it was coming from: we looked up and saw two small airplanes above us, flying dangerously low. We laughed nervously at our own stupidity for not being able to identify the sound of planes. This time, it was our turn to beckon to the villagers; we explained to them that they could come outside again and that we should have known better than to frighten them by panicking at the sound of planes overhead. But the worst was still to come.

The villagers refused to come out from their hiding places, and pointed to the skies above. Hundreds of mini-parachutes, each weighted down with something white and square, were descending upon us. We ran for dear life into the closest hut and watched the proceedings from positions of relative security. We were convinced they were bombs, but the question was, who would want to bomb peaceful little Kakumdo?

We didn't have to wait long for the answer. The tiny parachutes rained down on the village, hitting the square, the huts, the trees, the goat, everything in sight for about ten minutes. Then the noise subsided and all was quiet again. The villagers rushed out to grab the packages attached to the parachutes. We were more restrained as we gingerly stepped into the daylight again. Some of the packages had burst, spilling, of all things, powdered milk. There was mass jubilation and laughter as each group of villagers retrieved a bag of milk from somewhere around the village.

In the middle of this cacophony, a piercing wail was heard from the village square. We ran to see who was hurt, but instead we found a very old man, one of the previously laughing elders, clutching the still-tethered but by now very dead goat. The poor old man had spent his life's savings on the animal, knowing that it was the best invest-ment he could make—that goat would have provided his family with milk, manure, and baby goats that could be eaten or sold for extra money. Now packets of artificial milk descending from the sky had killed his natural milk provider. This was made all the more tragic as it transpired that the goat was pregnant.

The old man was inconsolable. Wailing pathetically, he kicked at the packets of milk lying close to him and clutched his dead goat in his arms. The villagers gathered around and stood helplessly watching.

This event made a powerful impression on me. Why didn't the people in the planes talk to the villagers before they dropped the milk? What if the villagers did not want or like milk? In what proportions were they to mix and prepare this powder with water in order to yield the correct concentration of milk? The instructions on the packages were in a foreign language, so why was there no one there to trans-late for the villagers? We felt hopelessly inadequate.

That single incident was, I believe, the beginning of my political conscience. I grew up.

✕✕✕ ▦▦ ✕ ✕ ▦▦

Of course, I had some more universal growing-up experiences too, although these too had a certain Ghanaian stamp to how they unfolded. Take the events of a certain day in sewing class.

It was one of Ghana's rare mild sunny days, and we would much rather have been outside on the school lawn, enjoying English Liter-ature lessons. Those lessons were like play for us, because we read about white peoples' history and lives, tales that—unlike our tradi-tional folk tales—seemed very abstract and removed from everyday experience. Studying *A Midsummer Night's Dream, The Devil's Disciple,* and *Lysistrata* was something like playing dress-up.

But our literature teacher had been sick for the past week, so instead of being outside, here we were, grudgingly sitting in a hot downstairs classroom taking sewing lessons. The teacher, Miss Quarcoo, was one of only a handful of black teachers at Wesley Girls, and we were torn between being nice to her and feeling frustrated because we would much rather be anywhere else but here.

I was particularly frustrated because I already knew most of the home economics curriculum, particularly the needlework and cooking. However, today promised to be a little different, as we were about to learn how to use a proper sewing machine. Every Ghanaian woman must have a sewing machine and know how to use it, as it is (or at least, has been) a vital part of a woman's dowry, so this was an important lesson.

I pondered the irony—Wesley Girls High School was supposed to have come so far from its original beginnings, with its reputation for training powerful women—and yet here we were, still learning needlework, bored out of our minds. I winced.

All week, I had been feeling a dull ache in my abdomen. I had basically ignored it, beyond resolving that on the weekend I would feast on okra stew with gari (cassava powder), beans, and chiles. It always did the trick when I had indigestion. Then I would follow it up with a visit to the house dispensary for some laxatives.

My mind was only half on the lesson. I wondered how long it would be before I could go to the toilet. My seat felt uncomfortable, and I was becoming convinced that I had wet myself.

Eventually, I plucked up the courage to ask Miss Quarcoo if I could be excused. Unfortunately, there was a line of girls at her desk, waiting for her to cut them a bit of fabric to practice on. I was feeling terribly self-conscious, and the line was moving very slowly. Finally, I called out from the back of the line, trying to remain as inconspicuous as possible.

"Uh, excuse me, Miss Quarcoo? May I please be excused from class for a moment?"

"Certainly, Charity. But first pick up your bit of fabric and give the machine a try. You can leave in five minutes."

I couldn't wait five minutes. Without a second thought, I dashed out of the room, and not even Miss Quarcoo's protests were strong enough to stop me. I reached the toilet, but my troubles had only begun. No one had prepared me for this. I was only thirteen years old and I was about to die in a stinking boarding-school toilet!

This was a logical assumption on my part—the only time my mum ever called an ambulance to the maternity home was when one of her patients was bleeding. But how was I going to alert anyone to call an ambulance from in here? There were no alarm bells, no phones in the toilet. Don't panic, I kept telling myself, you need to lose a lot of blood before you pass out and die.

I grabbed many layers of the hard toilet paper and fashioned a sort of padding for myself; an exercise in futility. This noisy translucent paper could not even absorb water, let alone anything else, but I had no alternative. I attempted to wash the back of my school uniform, which was soiled, and walked out dripping wet.

When I got back to class, I did not go in. I could not. Instead, I partially opened the door and signaled to Martha Badu to ask Miss Quarcoo to come to the door—it was an emergency. When Miss Quarcoo saw me, she seemed to know instinctively. She left one of the other girls in charge and walked me to my dormitory to change into dry clothes. Every step we took, the noisy toilet paper crunched and scratched in a rhythmic shuffle—crunch, scratch, crunch, scratch. I stopped walking. Miss Quarcoo must have sensed my embarrassment, because she slowed down and asked me to wait in the dormitory whilst she went to the dispensary. A few minutes later, she returned with several boxes of sanitary pads, and taught me how to use them. Not unreasonable for a home economics teacher, I guess, but why couldn't we have had these valuable lessons instead of so much sewing instruction?

The next day was Saturday. First thing in the morning, I went to the school office and called my mother. She didn't seem worried at all, even though I told her about the bleeding. Instead, she reassured me and said she'd write soon and send me a big parcel.

True to her word, the following week, my mother's parcel arrived. Now, when you're at boarding school, the thought of a package from home is uplifting indeed. But this package! She had sent me two packages of sanitary pads, a bottle of iron pills, a bottle of cod liver oil capsules, a container of multivitamins, and a long letter that dealt mostly with "now that you've grown-up" instructions on how to avoid contact with boys! She ended by promising me a traditional ceremonial dish of etor and egg on my next school holiday. This is a hard-boiled egg served atop a pointy mound of mashed yam colored with palm oil, which forms a sort of celebratory recognition of important life events.

I couldn't for the life of me understand what she was actually trying to say with her letter. After all, I was cooped up in an all-girls boarding school! If I never had much to do with boys when I was free and on holidays, where was I going to find the boys in here?

XXX XXX XX XX XXX

Certainly rank had its privileges and there were many advantages to being a member of Ghana's educated elite, but it didn't help any where meeting boys was concerned. I often wondered how different my life would have been, had I grown up in a traditional Ga setting.

Here I was, sixteen years old, a sophomore in high school, and my mother still would not allow me to go to a chaperoned school dance with boys; I couldn't even go to the annual Scripture Union meet, because there would be boys attending. In the meantime, my traditional Ga counterparts were preparing for a special celebration that takes place at set times throughout the year. The celebration is only for young people, and is called Otofo, which is a Southern Ghanaian tribal word for a young girl about to come of age.

During Otofo, all sixteen-year-old girls are ceremonially presented to the community, especially to the eligible young bachelors; it is a ritual statement and celebration of their availability. Life would have been so much easier if Wesley Girls High School had a ceremony like that.

The week before Otofo, the girls are given instruction to prepare them for their entry into adulthood. Aunties (meaning family friends) and older women of the family get together to indoctrinate them and answer any questions they may have about sexuality, sensuality, their bodies, and men. Basically they give them a kind of a workshop on how to be a woman, on the problems and advantages of being a woman, and on what they can expect from marriage.

Very early on the morning of the Otofo celebration, the girls are bathed with herbal water, whilst the women who wash them chant and sing, extolling the virtues of womanhood. The singing continues as the young maidens are polished from head to toe with lovely aromatic oils.

They wear a strapless wrap-around dress of white cotton, tied around the waist with a *duku,* or silk scarf duku. Golden bangles, as well as anklets and bracelets made of exotic trading beads strung with lumps of gold, adorn the girls' arms and legs. They are given special golden earrings and a ceremonial hairstyle, and their faces, arms, chests, shoulder blades and feet are painted with white tribal clay—*ayilor.*

And then the drummers start, playing intricate rhythms and singing amazing songs, praising the beauty of the Otofo maidens.

Accompanied by members of the family who are close to their age, the girls go from house to house, dancing for relatives and neighbors. Exotic food is hand-fed to the maidens throughout the day. In the afternoon, everyone gathers at one of the houses, where the girls perform the ritual Otofo dance and sing the song that declares their readiness to be known as a woman. The singing is accompanied by lively drumming and a delicate dance, choreographed to show off the nubile female form. The dancing girls are encouraged to take pride in their bodies and their coming of age as women.

OTOFO SONG

Kè nkèè Otofonyo dzimiee
If I say I'm a nubile young thing

Hamadalè ʃi
let me thank the gods

Otofonyo dzimiee, Hamadalè ʃi
If I say I'm a nubile young thing, let me thank the gods

Kaatsoo moni kewo no
If I'm shown the giver of my gifts

Hamadalè ʃi
let me thank the gods

Moni kewo no, Hamadalè ʃi
The giver of my gifts, let me thank the gods

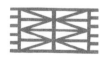

I WAS NEVER HERE...

Once, in the eastern region of Ghana, in the country town of Aburi, to be exact, in the hills far away from the coast, there lived a man named Yaw Adu. He was a simple man who had never been far from home, and spent his days farming and hunting. While he had heard travelers speak about the big city of Accra on the coast, and all the wondrous things to be found there, he had never been there—indeed, he had never been any farther from Aburi than to the surrounding mountains.

But one day Yaw's father sent him to Accra on business. Very excited, he put on his best clothes, and put his knife in his belt. Then he wrapped up some food in a piece of cloth, put it on his head, and set out on his way. He walked for many days, on a hot and dusty road. Eventually, he left his own region, and crossed over into a region where no one spoke Akwapim-twi, his language, any more.

As he got closer and closer to Accra, the road grew wider, and much, much busier. He saw more people and donkeys than he had ever seen before, as well as cars and timber trucks, all heading to and from the city.

Coming around a bend, he happened on a great herd of cows grazing by the edge of the road. He had never seen so many cows in one place in all his life, and he stopped and stared at them in wonder. When he finally spotted the little boy tending the herd, he went up to him and asked, "Who is the owner of all these cattle?"

But the little boy couldn't understand what Yaw was saying, as he didn't speak Akwapim-twi, so he looked up at the young man and answered, "Mini," which means "I don't understand what you mean" in the Ga dialect, which is what they speak around Accra.

"Mini! What a rich man this Mini must be to own so many cows!" Yaw said to himself.

He continued to travel down the road, and finally reached Accra itself. The city was more impressive than he had imagined in his wildest dreams, and he wandered around, soaking up the sights. On one street, he came upon a giant building, seemingly made of glass. There was nothing like this back in Aburi! Just then a woman passed by on her way to the marketplace, and Yaw said to her, "What a tremendous house! What person could be so rich as to own a place like this?"

But the woman didn't understand a word, as she couldn't speak Akwapim-twi, only Ga, and so she could only answer, "Mini."

"Mini! That man again! How astonishing!"

Yaw had never imagined anyone so wealthy. Certainly back in Aburi nobody had so many cows and such a big house. He decided to see what other wonders Accra held. Just then, he happened upon the marketplace. It covered a space larger than all of the houses in Aburi put together. As he walked amongst the stalls, he saw women selling things unheard of, or at least very rare, back home. Things like iron pots and drinking glasses. "Where do all these things come from?" Yaw asked a little girl.

She smiled shyly up at him and answered, "Mini."

Yaw couldn't believe it. Mini was everywhere. No wonder he was so rich.

As the day progressed the marketplace grew increasingly crowded. It was a big market day, and everyone for miles around had come to sell or buy. Yaw had never seen so many people in one place. Truly, he thought, the stories he had heard about Accra hadn't done it justice. He stopped an old man with a drum under his arm and asked him, "What is it with all of these people? Why are they all coming to Accra at the same time?"

"Mini," said the old man.

Yaw was truly overwhelmed now. What an amazingly influential man this Mini must be! Great crowds of people poured into Accra just because of him. And no one in Aburi had ever even heard of this great personage! How truly ignorant he and his fellow townspeople must be!

He left the crowds at the market and went down to the ocean shore. Here he saw a type of boat he'd never seen before, indeed a whole fleet of them, little fishing boats with writing on the sides.

"Eeeee! To whom do all these boats belong?" he asked a fisherman standing on the beach.

"Mini," the fisherman replied.

Yaw walked further down the beach and came to a dock where a giant iron cargo ship was being loaded with drums of palm oil and logs of timber. Thick black smoke spewed from its massive stacks, and hundreds of men swarmed over its decks.

"Ei!" cried Yaw to a man standing nearby with a huge bundle of plantains on his head. "This must be the biggest boat in the world."

"Mini?" the man replied.

"Well, yes, I'd guessed who owned it," Yaw said, "but where is all that timber going?"

"Mini," the man repeated, hopping up onto the ship's gangway.

Yaw was overcome with awe. Mini was an almost godlike man—he owned everything, he ate everything. It seemed you couldn't even ask a question without the city folk answering "Mini."

"I wouldn't believe it if I hadn't seen it," he said to himself. "They ought to call Accra Mini's town, for surely, he is everywhere. What must it be like to have so much wealth!"

Yaw then went and completed his business in Accra, wrapped some more food in his piece of cloth, and started out for home.

At the edge of the city, he came upon a great procession, and heard the beating of many drums. Drawing closer, he realized it was a funeral. Many men surrounded the coffin, lifting it high while throngs of women cried out in mourning. It was the most impressive funeral Yaw had ever seen. He pushed his way into the crowd and asked one of the mourners, "Who is this person who has died?"

"Mini," the mourner replied, sadly.

"What!" Yaw said, astonished, "the great Mini is dead? The man who owned the cattle and the tall house and the drinking glasses and the fishing boats and the steamship and the timber? The man whose very reputation has crowded the market square beyond belief? Oh, poor Mini. He had to leave all of this wealth behind. He died just like any ordinary person."

Yaw continued on out of the city, but he couldn't get the tragedy of Mini out of his mind.

"Poor Mini," he muttered to himself, over and over. "Poor Mini."

The Color of Underwear

"When a chicken finds itself in new terrain, it does not automatically stand on both feet at once."

AKAN PROVERB

Mum didn't really want me to go, but she had no choice. Once again, Aunt Sophie had come to my rescue. Without ever mentioning it to my mother, she'd paid the application fee for me to study Ophthalmic Nursing in Maidstone, Kent, England, and, out of the blue, a letter had arrived saying that I'd been accepted.

Aunt Sophie had a long talk with Mum. She reminded her of the promise I'd made to my grandfather to help people with vision problems, and told Mum that she'd arranged for me to stay with Gifty, Aunt Sophie's eldest daughter, who was living in Cricklewood, North London.

Finally, after much discussion, I left for London with a trunk full of pretty new outfits, all put together for me by my Aunty Betty, Aunt Sophie and Mum. I was heading out, another powerful Wesley Girl off to make my mark on the world.

Not that all of the skills I acquired at Wesley Girls were equally useful out there in the real world. The self-confidence and ability to deal with many different people in many different situations stood me in good stead, but the etiquette lessons were something of a different story.

Take the manner in which we were taught to eat soup. Now, in our culture, we Ghanaian girls had learned how to eat soup daintily using nothing but our fingers, so the idea of a complex set of rules was a great amusement to us. And complex they were, indeed.

According to our very earnest white instructors, a refined young lady is supposed to sit at the dinner table upright, her feet "elegantly deposited on the ground," with no crossing of the knees or ankles. The proper distance for a body from the dinner table is no more, and no less, than three inches. Her torso should be at a right angle to her thighs, and she is expected to have her hands placed sensibly in her lap. As she prepares to eat her soup, she must lean towards the dinner table at approximately a 30-degree angle, using her right hand to pick up the soup spoon.

Holding the bowl with her left hand, she is to carefully tilt it away from her (approximately 10 to 15 degrees), while the little finger of her right hand rests on the edge of the bowl. Still holding the bowl with her left hand, she releases her right hand from the bowl, turning the spoon so that the scoop is facing away from her. Now she fills the spoon until it is one-third to half-full and then slowly, keeping the spoon steady with her thumb, index finger and middle finger, she extends her little finger again as she raises the spoon to her lips, simultaneously lowering the bowl slowly down to its original position. She should then put her left hand back down in her lap and lean her torso (while still holding the spoonful of soup carefully) a further ten degrees forward towards the spoon. Of course, ladies with larger breasts were expected to lean a little bit less forward, so that her bosoms didn't end up in the soup!

I WAS NEVER HERE...

Vital to the success of proper soup consumption was the correct puckering of lips—it was recommended that the "O" of the pucker be approximately the size of a shilling. Lifting the spoon to her lips, the lady should slowly tip the contents into her mouth without slurping or spilling, after which she daintily dabs the corners of her mouth with a napkin.

This is all very well if you have Caucasian lips, but when we full-lipped African children puckered up to the size of a shilling to tip our soup in, we'd end up spilling it all over ourselves. Now, if we had been asked to pucker up into two shillings, we might have stood a better chance. Instead, this etiquette lesson turned into a total disaster.

Another important skill we learned in etiquette class was how to pick up a man. As well-brought-up ladies, we were taught that we must, at all times, have in our possession square white handkerchiefs. The lace of the handkerchief should be on one corner only and below the lace we were to have our monogrammed initials; lace going all around the handkerchief was a definite sign of bad breeding.

You were supposed to fold the hanky, much as a man folds a hand-kerchief for his vest pocket, then hold it together with both hands so that the lace poked out of the top. It was supposed to make a lady look very angelic, what with only her monogrammed initials and the beautiful bit of lace appearing above her clasped hands.

If the lady sees a man she likes, she should stand where she is, clasping her little handkerchief, and follow him around the room with her eyes until he finally notices her. It never occurred to us that the poor girl might stand there for hours, rooted to the spot, unnoticed by the man she fancied!

Anyway, the idea is that eventually the lucky young man will notice her and, when he does, she should avert her eyes coyly, looking discreetly down at the floor. With her head still bowed down a little and her chin low, she must smile very sweetly and then, keeping her head in that position, slowly elevate her eyes back to his face. This is

At Wesley Girls High School—sweet 16 and never been kissed!

I WAS NEVER HERE...

guaranteed to make him go absolutely mad. She now keeps her eyes glued to him and keeps the smile on her face. I have noticed that Princess Diana does this very well.

After a reasonable amount of time, if her man still doesn't realize that she is burning with passion for him, she is permitted to flick open her handkerchief by the lace and shake it gently, all the while keeping her gaze on him. Lifting her handkerchief slowly with her right hand, she should drop it daintily over her right shoulder as she flounces off, leaving it there in the hope that he might run forward, pick it up and say "I say AR (noticing the monogram on her hand-kerchief), I believe you dropped something."

This strategy will enable her to strike up a charming conversation with him, which he will no doubt see as an opportunity to broach the serious subject of dating.

Now, what with all my mother's concern about my meeting boys, and the fairly rigid traditional structures governing how such things are supposed to occur in my culture, I had never had a chance to try this surefire method.

I had scarcely been in London a week when I got my opportunity. It was a cold December morning and I needed to do a bit of shopping. Well, no sooner had I entered the little supermarket on Cricklewood High Street than I caught sight of a gorgeous black man standing in the produce section. I thought to myself, Wow, I could easily baby-sit this one forever! Best of all, my mother was not around.

And, lo and behold, being a well-brought-up lady, I had on me a white handkerchief monogrammed with the lace in the right spot. I immediately employed my sophisticated handkerchief-clutching, eye-rolling, pick-up technique. No response. So, gazing at the man with a sickly sweet smile, I flicked my handkerchief over my right shoulder, turned with a little flounce, and walked away. Nobody called out to me. Nothing. I'd walked a whole block before I finally turned around. The man was nowhere to be seen and my beautiful white handkerchief had been trodden underfoot by all the passers by.

I was heartbroken. I ran to Gifty's flat, threw myself on my bed and cried, then sat down to write a letter to my mother.

December 24, 1965

Dear Mum,

London is awful. The English have no manners whatsoever.

※◇※ ⅲ ※ ※ ⅲ

England was full of surprises.

One afternoon, as I was looking through the weekend paper, I saw an advertisement for flesh-colored underwear. Up until that moment I had never had to buy my own underwear. Never. They always just kind of miraculously appeared on my bed whenever I needed new ones, whether at home or at boarding school. But today, I cut the advertisement from the paper and headed off to Marks and Spencer, the local department store where the sale was being held.

After half an hour of looking through all the different styles of panties, trying to find the flesh-colored underwear, I still hadn't found any. I went over to the sales assistant and said, "I believe you've got flesh-colored underwear on sale here. Can you tell me where I can find them?"

"Have a look in aisle two in the bargain baskets."

I had already been through everything in aisle two, but I thought I'd give it another try, just in case.

At that moment, a little girl at the other end of the shop pointed in my direction and said, "Oh Mummy, look at the lady with the black face!"

I thought there might have been a clown or some sort of mime with a painted face behind me and I turned around to look, but there

I WAS NEVER HERE…

was no one there. I figured I must have missed her and didn't think anything more of it, then returned to my search for the flesh-colored underwear.

I went back to the sales assistant and said, "Look, I can't find them. I'm not sure if I'm looking in the right place."

She said, "Oh no, you do want aisle two. They're probably just down at the bottom of the basket. Have another look and if you still can't find any, I'll come and help you."

So I went back and I looked. Slightly embarrassed, I returned to the sales assistant. "I'm not trying to be difficult, but I really am having a bit of trouble locating your flesh-colored underwear."

The sales lady came with me to aisle two, lifted a pair of salmon-pink panties up to me and said, "Here they are—"

As the reality dawned on both of us, we dissolved into spontaneous laughter.

In the meantime, the little girl in the shop had walked closer to us with her mother. She came up and touched me and said, "See, Mummy, there's the lady with the black face."

My natural instinct was to ask the sales assistant, "Is my mascara running?"

She said "No, no. In England we call dark-skinned people black."

Her comment wiped the laughter clean off my face. I can't even remember the reply I gave. Absolutely amazed and overwhelmed by the whole thing, I simply said, "Thank you very much," and walked away.

Back home in the security of my room, I sat in front of the mirror, staring at myself and thinking, I suppose I must be black. I never really thought of myself as such. I just thought of myself as me, you know? I discovered a whole range of emotions that day, and there were many more to come.

In order to broaden our work opportunities, the ophthalmic nursing program recommended its students also train as general registered nurses. I was happy to do so, and our training hospital's matron, or nurse administrator, helped me and a girl named Irene Chapman to apply for our general nursing training at St. George's Hospital in London. We were invited to have an interview and, believe it or not, an IQ test.

After the interview, Irene and I were sat in a room with thick stacks of papers. I had grown accustomed to taking exams at Wesley Girls, so the IQ test didn't faze me. In fact, it looked sort of fun—putting things in boxes, choosing the odd one out, all that sort of thing. A few weeks later, a letter arrived saying that Irene passed, while I, and I quote, "had failed abysmally."

Elvira, the matron, was as shocked as I. Luckily, we had just received the results of our Ophthalmic Nursing exams, on which I had performed brilliantly. Elvira wrote to St. George's requesting that they send her a copy of my test. They replied that, unfortunately, they had destroyed the exam results, but would be happy to offer me another exam if I was willing to come back to London.

This time, Elvira accompanied me to St. George's. I took the second exam and, of course, two weeks later a letter arrived saying that my test scores had gone from abysmal to excellent. A few months later, they took me into St. George's to train as their first black State Registered Nurse.

The Straw That Almost Broke My Back

Student nurses at St. George's were rotated through all of the hospital's branches, in order to ensure that we got a well-rounded education. And we did it all—pediatrics, gynecology, neurosurgery, and psychiatry. While studying the latter, I caught the eye of a psychiatric registrar who lectured third-year student nurses, Dr. Julian Hafner (and I didn't even use a handkerchief to do so!). The nurses' home was only about 200 yards from the hospital, but he would follow me at the curb in his little blue MG convertible, calling out "Can I give you a lift? I would like to talk to you. You look very lovely today. Perhaps I can carry your bags for you?" I always ignored him, partly because I was shy and partly because I was already dating someone and didn't want to complicate things.

After my stint on the psychiatric ward ended, I ran into him a couple other times and once, slightly tipsy at a party, he said that he would like to take me out sometime. But I was pretty straightlaced, and I figured that any man who would ask you out when he was under the influence didn't really mean it. But life moves in funny ways sometimes, and so it was that some three years after our first encounters,

I ended up married to Julian who was, by then, a researcher and honorary senior registrar at the Maudsley Hospital, London.

Everything went pretty well at first, although his family wasn't too happy that their golden boy was marrying some black girl from Africa. Of course, it never occurred to them that as far as my parents were concerned, I was their little golden girl, and they too had issues with the marriage. Not so much because Julian was white, because my family was multiracial and never saw things in terms of color, but because they were afraid that if I married a foreign person they might never see me again.

On our first anniversary, we got into a horrible fight. We had gone out dancing, and drank perhaps a little bit too much champagne. Perhaps a lot too much. Somehow we got on the subject of families, and Julian said, quite calmly, that he didn't want to have children. Well, I was shocked. Shocked! I loved this man and we had been living together for eighteen months before we got married. Half drunk, I got up and walked out on him, my mind awhirl with thoughts. I was a career girl. I had grown up in a matriarchy. I didn't need him or any man. In fact, the only reason I'd married him was because I didn't want my children, our children, who were obviously going to be mixed-race, to grow up with the additional problem of not having a legal father. I resolved to see a lawyer first thing in the morning and get out of this ridiculous marriage.

All this went through my head in only two blocks, before I heard footsteps. Julian was running after me, calling out, "Don't be silly. I'm just a bit drunk. We're both drunk. Of course we can have babies. Of course we want to have babies. We can start tonight." I thought he sounded demented, and I kept walking.

We walked and talked all night; by the time we got back to the disco it was seven in the morning, and neither one of us could remember where we'd parked the car. In fact, we were so anxious to get home

18 years old and an opthalmic nurse in England.

and start making babies that we took a cab home and did just that.

Nine months to the day after that fight, I was scheduled to be induced for labor. The pregnancy had been extremely difficult, as I'd had recurring fibroid uterine tumors, and had been hospitalized several times. Thus, I was really worried about the health of my baby, and filled with trepidation about the whole process. And, as a nurse, I knew there were all sorts of things that could go wrong.

The night before the baby was due, however, I went into labor. By the morning the pains were not high enough or fast enough, but I was still admitted into the hospital so that the doctors could encourage the labor process.

Now I had worked in Kings College Hospital's intensive care unit as a relief nursing sister, so I knew the system and the hospital very well, and Julian came with me. A guided pump was attached to the baby's head and then attached to the monitor, and I was given a syntocinon drip, but because they knew that I was a nursing sister they turned the volume down on the monitor that monitored the baby's heartbeat and they turned the screen away from me so I didn't have to see anything, and they went off. They didn't want me checking the monitor for problems; they wanted me to be as relaxed as possible.

The sister came in and said, "I'm going to have a few meetings and do the ward rounds and I'll be back." As the senior staff midwife, she told the staff midwives to keep an eye on me and I heard her say to them in subdued tones, "There is a senior staff specialist's wife having a baby here in this ward. Take good care of her because we have had a few problems with her pregnancy and so we wouldn't want anything else to be going wrong now would we? I will have a cup of coffee as well and I will be back."

There were two of us women in the labor ward at that time, me and a white woman lying across the room on the bed. Now, the nursing staff must have thought that the senior staff specialist's wife referred to was the woman across the room from me because I saw them massaging her back with powder and turning her over in the bed, giving her extra pillows, fetching her drinks, and so on. I thought that the poor thing must be really ill; I even offered her my magazines to read because I felt sorry for her.

While all this was going on, a black foreign doctor (the visiting anesthetist) was brought in. She had come to King's College Hospital to learn how to give epidurals (a type of spinal anesthesia). They walked over to me, turned me over, and said that this doctor was going to give me an epidural. I protested furiously, saying, "No, I don't need an epidural. I'm not written down for one and I don't want one." It was an option that I had been offered during my interview, and if my pain got really bad I would have had one, but I wasn't prepared for one, nor did I want or need one.

They condescendingly reassured me, "No, don't worry about it. I think the time has come for us to give you one."

I said, "I think you have got the wrong patient."

They took no notice of me: "This doctor will be very kind and very gentle."

They had obviously decided that there's a black doctor here and she must practice on a black person and so they didn't listen to me. There I was having a baby on the table and this woman was practicing her medical techniques. She started the procedure and I heard her mutter under her breath, "Oh, CSF" (cerebral spinal fluid)—she had gone into the wrong space in my back. It really hurt, and I felt a shockingly bad headache shooting down the back of my neck. I kept telling them how much pain I was in but they took no notice and kept reassuring me. I could hear her muttering under her breath, "CSF."

I then said, "Look, I didn't come in here to have a lumbar puncture. I came in here to have a baby. I don't want an epidural."

They said, "No, no, calm down, don't get agitated, Mrs. Hafner.

This doctor will look after you. She will get it into the right space, don't worry."

They refused to accept that I was a nursing sister, a colleague of theirs, and that I actually knew what was going on. Anyway, the long and short of it was that I started hearing ringing in my ears and my hearing was going. I could see the staff's mouths moving but I couldn't hear them and I told them this but they still took no notice and then my vision started to go and I kept telling them that I couldn't see them.

The whole thing of the nightmare took about fifteen minutes but for me it was like eternity and the thing that hurt me most was that the man that I loved so much, my husband and the baby's father, who was holding onto me, was asked to leave. "Mr. Hafner," one of the staff said, "it is very hard for us to do our work efficiently while you are in here with us so would you mind stepping outside of the door and if we have any complications we'll call you."

I screamed for him not to go. I begged him, "Don't leave me. I'm frightened. I don't know what they are going to do to me." He tried to calm me. "Don't worry, you're just panicking. The epidural will go well." I said, "But Julian I don't want an epidural. You know that." He said, "Well obviously they have decided that it is the best thing for you." He reassured me and then left me.

Well, by the time I got my vision and my hearing back the senior staff midwife had got back from her meetings, ward rounds, and cof-

fee break and was ready to take charge again. She turned up the volume of my monitor. I knew immediately that something was seriously wrong and that my baby was in fetal distress because the monitor went "beepbeepbeepbeepbeep," very fast. She turned to the other midwives and demanded to know what had been going on. "Where is Dr. Hafner...Mrs. Hafner's husband, the senior staff specialist?" The midwives turned crimson but were too shocked to speak. They finally understood what they had done.

The senior midwife turned to me and said, "I'm terribly sorry, Dorinda, there has been a little mix-up. I don't need to lie to you. The epidural was not supposed to be for you. It was for the other lady and now your baby has gone into fetal distress. We must not waste time. We have to operate immediately, give you a cesarean in the next few minutes. Don't worry, we'll save your baby."

I was livid. I felt betrayed, but I didn't know what else I could do, so I agreed. They said I had to sign a consent form. I said, "I want to know who is going to give me the anesthetic, and I want to see my doctor and my husband."

Dr. Elias came and reassured me that everything would go well. I signed the form. My husband was there. They took me into the operating room. I thought, *good, at least something good is going to happen to me.* I was going to get my baby and all would be well.

In those days in order to give you a general anesthetic you were given an oxygen mask and encouraged to take a deep breath of oxygen first so that there was enough oxygen going through your blood stream while they intubated you before they attached you to the rest of their machines. They gave me a black and white mask and said, "Take a deep breath of oxygen." I did and I said, "Oh, no, it's not oxygen." They argued with me and said, "No, no, no, calm down. You are excited at the moment because of what's happened before—you've been traumatized. It is oxygen."

So I said, "Here you are. You take a deep breath for me and tell me it is oxygen." The anesthetist took a deep breath from it and he went white. He said, "You're right. It's not oxygen. It's halothane."

Well, that was it. I went bananas. I pulled out the intravenous tubes from my arm and I screamed and yelled. I went absolutely hysterical. Dr. Elias came and calmed me down and talked to me and I said, "I don't trust these people. They are going to kill me."

He was eventually able to calm me down, and I was put under anesthetic. I came out of it all with a healthy baby. Apparently, from what I'm told, I woke up briefly after the cesarean. As soon as I heard that the baby didn't have red hair, I went straight back to sleep. My great-grandpa had had red hair, and I spent nine months worrying that I'd have a black kid with red hair. We call them "ofligyato," and they get teased mercilessly by other kids.

During the following week, while I was recovering in my hospital bed and getting acquainted with James, my new son, a deputation came to see me. It included Dr. Elias, two anesthetists, their senior staff midwife, and another midwife. They had come to ask me if I was going to make a fuss about the events that occurred in the labor ward and operating room. In fact they went as far as asking me to think carefully and refrain from making any accusations or taking it further and they wanted assurance from me that I wouldn't.

I couldn't give them what they wanted, because I had no idea what lasting effects those drugs and that impromptu epidural might have on my life. I was concerned that I might not even be fit and healthy enough to look after my baby. But I never filed any sort of action, partly because Julian discouraged me and partly because I had no immediate pain. I experienced severe pain in my spine much, much later when it was too late to confront them.

To this day, when I get very tired I have problems with my spine, and a tendency to get these odd spasms, a dragging feeling that forces me to arch my back and hold my head and feet still until it passes. I have no doubt that this is a direct result of that day in the labor ward so many years ago and so far away from Aunty Thelma's, where such a thing could never have taken place.

Back in Ghana, the birth of a child is rarely such a trauma. The troubles seem to come earlier, particularly when the pregnancy is announced. I recall that my mother didn't just help bring a lot of children into the world, she also helped a number of them find their parents. You see, back home, just about every married man I knew had a second wife, a concubine, or worse, a lover on the side. A number of the single girls I knew had given birth to babies, and some of those were not entirely sure who the father was. This was common enough that in my youth I had several times witnessed the ceremony commonly referred to as Asking The Way To The Father's House.

The ceremony involved summoning elders from both the pregnant girl's and any male suspect's families to a dawn gathering, usually held at the home of the girl. Children were not supposed to witness these meetings, which might help explain why they were held at such an ungodly hour.

When we were little, my cousin Theresa and I had a secret hiding spot in a small room adjacent to the living room, which was separated by glass shutter windows. We could hide behind the curtains and both peek into the sitting room and hear the conversations. We would listen intently as the elders exchanged big tribal words, words we had never heard spoken in everyday language, but which we deciphered to mean only rude or sexy things. Occasionally, the arguments got nasty and the elders were moved to fight when they thought somebody present had slurred the name of their angelic child.

The common though unspoken understanding was that boys would be boys, and would and should roam, but good girls should remain virtuous enough not to allow *any* boy to have his way with them. Thus, the two sides presented arguments that generally could be summed up as (1) the girl was a temptress or (2) the boy was a raving Casanova who had deceived an innocent maiden. In these matters, gray areas did not exist.

My cousin Sarah had been just thirteen years old when she got pregnant. I'd not even noticed any change in her, so it came as a horrible shock to see the elders sitting in the family sitting room at dawn discussing her future. The arguments raged forwards and backwards in hushed tones.

"Whose child is it anyway?" my mother had asked. Mum had been close to tears as she explained to the gathered assembly how she felt let down by Sarah, since she is her brother's child from his first wife.

My uncle had fifteen children from his two wives. Although Mum was younger than her brother, she had nonetheless felt duty bound, as is customary for the oldest female sibling, to help out by looking after one of her brother's children. She'd picked Sarah because Sarah showed academic promise and was the eldest girl. My mum felt that she could give Sarah an education and thereby make her a role model for the younger kids. Sarah was supposed to provide incentive, especially for the girls. And now this!

Sarah did have a boyfriend, and I could hear the accused boy's father denying that his son was capable of such an atrocity. He was outraged, because for his son to impregnate such a young girl, a girl above his station *and* of a different tribal background would be a major calamity. But hadn't Mum herself commented on how bright this boy was, and as a result of this high opinion obtained for him an apprenticeship with a carpenters' firm? And had his family not been so full of gratitude that they'd sent Mum a bounty from their farm: yams, cassava, plantains, tomatoes, bunches of spinach, two white chickens, and two dozen eggs? The families had both been very happy when the boy had been enterprising enough to develop a business opportunity between his carpenter bosses and his father's timber plantation. Yes, the father was very pleased with his boy and he found this whole inci-

dent totally distasteful and quite out of character. He reminded everybody that you never bite the hand that feeds you.

The boy's aunty, Madam Akosua Mansah, who had been quiet
throughout most of the proceedings, agreed with her brother, the boy's
father. Yes, their boy was good. So good, in fact, that he even drove all
the local kids to church on Sundays and afterwards took it upon himself to teach Sarah and the other girls, who liked to play with corn dolls,
how to make them. Poor Aunty didn't realize that by trying to save the
boy's skin, she had actually implicated him further. Nonetheless, all of
the boy's family was in agreement, he was a good young man.

But then, as if to muddy the waters further, the boy's Uncle
Oppong Boateng threw a wrench in the works. Didn't Sarah and her
cousin (meaning me) twice a week spend several hours in the rooms
of one Mr. Dawson, the math teacher, who happened to be a fellow
tenant in the house the family rented at Krofrom? Had not Mum
herself insisted that Mr. Dawson tutor the girls in math? So how
were they to know that Sarah's pregnancy wasn't because of Mr.
Dawson? And worse, what if Mr. Dawson had also been tampering
with both girls?

I gasped so loudly that I nearly betrayed our hiding place. Had
not a cock crowed at that very instant, I would have been discovered
and soundly smacked.

How could Uncle Oppong Boateng throw a red herring into such
a serious argument? I was furious, adults really were idiots. I thought,
No wonder the kids call you "pong pong" behind your back. You are
indeed a fool. It doesn't take an A student to know that Mr. Dawson
is old enough to be our father. Besides, I thought, the very fact that
he was a math teacher should disqualify him. Who can imagine a
math teacher with a sex life? And he is so-o-o old, already married,
with a big grown-up family. Worse, he is *ananta* or knock-kneed; in
our society, only desperate people would make love to a knock-kneed

person, since the condition is ridiculed and seen as unusually unattractive. Clearly this uncle had a sick mind!

Someone else in the room cited the boy across the road who came to chop the family's firewood as another possible culprit. At this point it all became too much for my mum. The slur on her niece, her daughter, her family name and finally, the insinuation that Sarah could have been intimate with several boys, sent shock waves through her.

You always knew when Mum was near to explosion. She would stand, draw herself up to her full, imposing height, look to the ceiling, and then slowly, deliberately walk up and down whatever space was available, measuring her steps carefully as if she were scared of treading on baby chicks. It was a mistake to let this seeming composure fool you; one wrong word from anyone and she'd swat them like a fly from the air. She could be lethal on these occasions.

On this morning, she rose up just like that and started pacing up and down in front of the gathered elders. All eyes were upon her.

Three whole minutes went by, everyone watching tensely. Sailing regally down the center of the gathering, she finally spoke, picking her words like a judge about to read a death sentence. I had never seen my mother more sharp, like she had received the Ten Commandments on the mountain instead of Moses, her eyes narrowed to slits, her jaw set and her lips pursed.

Without warning, she swooped down on the tray of hot tea served as a polite gesture to the elders when they first arrived. In one continuous action, she grabbed a teaspoon from the tray with one hand and handed it to the boy's bewildered father; with her other hand she snatched my cousin Sarah from the low stool where she had been sitting quietly next to my mother's own vacated seat, thrusting her forward towards the father's feet. The action sent Sarah prostrate on the floor, as though in supplication. Sarah was too shocked to move. She lay still, face down.

Then Mum spoke, addressing the father directly. "Seeing that you and your family have all seen fit to slur my daughter's name and brand my niece as a whore with insinuations that she must have slept with not one but several men, perhaps as the father of this recalcitrant boy you might care to take this spoon and scoop out which of the offending sperms belong to your son!"

A stunned silence fell upon the elders as mouths gaped open. Nobody moved.

I was so proud of her. What a woman, what wisdom. I had read in the Bible about King Solomon, but Mum's reply today topped the lot. It was all I could do not to applaud with excitement.

The boy's family realized that they'd been beaten. Finding their voices again, they agreed to wait until the baby was born, after which they'd return with the obligatory bottles of alcoholic spirits and some money to do the right thing by giving the baby a name and showing it the way to its father's house.

Sarah died this year after twenty years and nine children with that boy. May she rest in peace.

Aren't You in Psychiatry?

s is the way of this book, and any story about a life, we now jump a few years, skipping over the premature birth of my daughter, Nuala, to another big crisis point that tested my strength. What, you might ask, would make a perfectly sane African woman living in England want to uproot herself, not to mention her two kids and her husband, giving up everything she has come to know and love in her adopted country to live 10,000 miles away in Australia?

My husband and I had been happy enough in England. My work as an optician was going quite well, and Julian's position as senior staff specialist (or consultant, as they are known in England) in psychiatry at St. George's Hospital was equally secure. It was just that, like everybody else at the time, we needed a change. We dreamed of greener pastures, different professional possibilities, and a better climate for ourselves, our two-year old son and our rather wheezy, struggling one-year old daughter. And then the opportunity to emigrate presented itself right out of the blue.

Julian had worked with an Australian doctor years before, at a London teaching hospital, and now this man had been appointed to a chair at the newly opened Flinders University of South Australia. My husband's colleague had decided he would assemble his own team of medical experts, people he knew he could trust and work with closely, and made Julian an offer he couldn't refuse.

Now, in the 1970s Australia's immigration policy makers were not exactly sending out invitations for black people to hop on the next ship sailing for the Land Down Under, even if they were of British nationality, as I was at the time. Still, we were quite taken aback when the Tasmanian immigration official interviewing us at Australia House in London pointedly explained that our choice of Adelaide, South Australia as a base was not entirely wise, and recommended Sydney or Melbourne as the more cosmopolitan and hence less racially problematic. We explained that that just wouldn't work, given the job offer, and eventually prevailed. On November 1, 1977, we arrived in Adelaide with baggage and children in tow.

We had been living in Australia for about two years when it began to occur to me that all was not well. Well, actually, my first clue came when I attended a meeting for the wives of senior staff specialists. A little club had been formed for these doctors' wives, designed to give them an outlet to socialize with other adults, since most of us at the time were at home with young children. As a newcomer, I was invited along to make me feel at home and accepted, and I eagerly got myself down to the university common room where the meeting was to be held one evening.

We all sat in a circle, and the smiling hausfraus introduced themselves in turn, moving around the circle. "Hello, my name is Mary Brierson and I'm in surgery," "Good evening, my name is Pamela Brown and I'm in gynecology," "How do you do, I'm Martha Peterson and I'm in research...."

I sat there feeling totally inadequate and thinking, My God, the room is full of academics. What am I going to say when it gets to me? I thought, Ah, well, I can only tell the truth.

When it was my turn to introduce myself, I said, "Good evening ladies, my name is Dorinda Hafner, and I want to thank you so much for inviting me. I am a trained nursing sister and a dispensing optician, but I have also done some acting and several TV commercials."

Everybody turned to look at me with varying degrees of surprise and horror. Finally, somebody broke the silence.

"No you're not. Aren't you in psychiatry? Isn't that what your husband does?"

All these women had been defining themselves according to what their husbands did! As the product of a matrilineal society, this was unimaginable to me. In Ghana, not only do women not necessarily take their husband's names upon marriage, they also take pride in running their own businesses. Indeed, we have a saying in Ghana: "His money is for all of you, and your money is for you." This was how I had always understood things to stand in the world. Yet here I was in an apparently modern civilization, sitting among intelligent women who seemed to have no self. I stuck to my guns, saying, "No, he's in psychiatry, I am who I said I am."

With forced politeness, they let it pass. And, for lack of anything better to do, I stayed in the club. One of the wives' long-standing traditions was to host dinner parties for visiting academics; each of the wives took a turn hosting the dinner, depending on whether the particular academic was visiting her husband's department or not. I managed to escape this particular duty for a few years, but finally one of my fellow club members cornered me. "Look madam," she said, "everybody else has done this dinner thing two or three times except you. How about hosting a dinner party for the professor from Newcastle University who's scheduled to visit your husband's department?"

What could I say? I knew that they would all expect me to cook African dishes, so I decided to show off my culinary versatility by preparing a seven-course French menu. I desperately needed to prove to these people that I could do things their way, as well as my own way, and in most cases, better.

THE MENU

Crudités with Garlic Cream

French Onion Soup and Fresh Miniature Bread Rolls

Salmon Soufflé

Filet de Boeuf En Croute with Spinach Steamed in Orange Juice

Crème Caramel and Brandy-flamed Crêpes Suzettes cooked
    at the table

Cheeses and Fresh Fruits

Freshly Ground Coffee

After Dinner Mints/Rum Truffles

We ate well that night. Conversations were lively and laughter plenty. All went well. That is, until the coffee.

After the cheese and fruit had been enjoyed, I slipped into the kitchen to bring together the last course. I arranged the jug of hot coffee, a smaller jug of plain hot water, cream, milk, sugar, and the coffee cups, saucers and teaspoons on a wide, silver tray in the kitchen. I was using my favorite crockery, an elegant black coffee set reserved for special occasions. I was out to impress and this was to be my pièce de résistance. The mints and chocolates were on a smaller, separate tray, decoratively arranged with flowers.

I surveyed the trays; everything was as it should be. I drew a deep satisfied breath and lifted my exquisite arrangement. Now, I suppose I must have spilled something on the floor previously without realizing it, because I only took two steps before I felt my feet slide out from under me. As my legs folded, the only thing I could think was Do not spill the coffee! Do not burn your stomach!

I hung onto the tray, braced for grim death, until I landed flat on my back on the floor, with a mighty thud. A pain shot thorough my pelvis and I lay motionless, breathing rapidly and in some considerable pain.

When I was able to focus, I was pleased to note that, with the exception of a few spills, my tray of coffee and goodies was intact. I sighed with relief. Just then, the dividing door to the dining room opened. My guests must have head the commotion, and sent Julian in to check on me.

My husband stood in the kitchen, looking scornfully down at me on the floor. Slowly, he bent over and lifted the full tray from my stomach, where it had come to rest. He squinted at me and, disdainfully, said, "I always knew you wanted to break this coffee set. You hate it because my sister gave it to us!" And with that helpful bit of free psychoanalysis, he turned round with the tray and went in to serve the coffee.

It took about ten minutes before I was sufficiently able to crawl on all fours to our bedroom—an eternity. I called for a doctor to come and check me over, despite the fact that there were four medical specialists in my living room.

In retrospect, I see that this was the turning point in our marriage—although I stayed with Julian for another three years, battling our various inner and outer devils. That night, as my back throbbed with pain, I thought about my background, about the strong women I had known growing up, and the strong woman I knew I was, and it seemed ridiculous that I had allowed myself to come to this juncture.

Lying there alone in my bed in Australia, I had the weight of thousands of years of African tradition telling me that women are strong and clever and capable, that you don't need a man to survive. As soon as I got off my back, I was going to have to stand on my own two feet.

I was ready for a change.

I WAS NEVER HERE...

L ong ago in a village in Ashanti, there lived a very beautiful girl named Abena. She was so beautiful, in fact, that all the young men for miles around would come to her house to court her. But alas, she had a bitter tongue, and the more ardently they praised her, the ruder she was to them.

To one she would say, "How could I marry you? You are so thin, no one could respect you as a man," and to the next, "I can't marry you, you are too fat. How could you possibly do any work?"

She scoffed at the hunters as uncivilized people, and at the farmers for being covered in dirt. The poor men were, of course, unacceptable due to their poverty, and the rich men she invariably found to be ugly or ill-mannered.

Abena's mother was a good, humble woman, and she found her daughter's behavior absolutely shameful. She pleaded constantly with Abena to choose one of the worthy suitors who sought her hand, saying, "Who are you my daughter to be so high and mighty? We may be a good, solid family, but we are hardly Ashanti royals! Have not all of your ancestors come from this village? Why must you so shame our family?"

But Abena just laughed and, when the nephew of a big chief from a neighboring town came to woo her, she was especially cruel, sending the boy away very angry.

Now, some ways away on the banks of a river lived a very large python who happened to have magical powers. He heard of Abena's great beauty and vicious humor, and decided that it would amuse him greatly to win her hand in marriage. He slithered toward the village and, when he was nearly there, he turned himself into a handsome prince, dressed in cloth of gold. As this vision walked through the village the people stared at his beauty and bowed down before him.

When he reached Abena's house, he asked her parents if he might see her. Now, Abena was in her room admiring herself in a mirror when her parents called her out to meet this handsome stranger. She came out sulky and reluctant, but when she saw the prince, her face lit up. Without even waiting to be asked, the radiant girl told her parents that at last she had found the man she wished to marry.

The prince paid Abena many compliments, and asked her if he could marry her at once. He was so charming that her parents couldn't say no—not that that was likely to begin with! After all, they'd begun to fear that she would never agree to a match. The prince showered them with gold, and soon the wedding festivities were under way.

After the ceremonies, the prince asked Abena's parents to gather together as much food as they could, because the journey to his palace was a long one, and they would surely need it on the way. So the parents gathered many sheep, pigs, and goats, as well as bushels and baskets of cassava, yam, plantain, and other fruits and vegetables. And they called thirty young maidens to help carry the food for the newlyweds.

The party started off well enough, but as soon as they had left the village—but not even cleared the surrounding farms—the prince asked them to stop, as he was hungry and needed a meal. Then he swallowed four goats, a sheep, a basket of yams, and a pineapple for dessert.

They continued on their way, Abena a little less arrogant than she'd been at the outset, but still trying to put a good face on things. Two hours later, the prince again called the little procession to a halt, as he was hungry. This time, he consumed three sheep, a pig, and all the bananas. And then they contined with their journey, as before.

And sure enough, as before, two hours later, the prince was hungry again. He ate all the baby lambs, two goats, some pawpaw, and a sack of corn. And they went on their way.

And so it went all day. Abena's high spirits evaporated entirely as she watched her husband eat. At last she said, "My dearest husband, if you go on eating like this, we'll run out of food long before the end of our journey."

"I can't help it," he said, "I'm hungry. A man has to eat!"

Soon he had indeed eaten all of the food, but in two hours, he called a halt anyway, asking for another meal. When Abena told him there was no more food, he said, "Then I guess I'll have to eat the maids."

By the end of the second day, the prince had eaten everything but Abena and himself. Luckily, they soon arrived at the river. When they reached its banks, the prince showed Abena a big hole in the ground, under the roots of a large tree. "That is the entrance to my palace," he told her. "Go on in and make yourself at home."

Abena was speechless. "My love," she said, "surely you must be joking. Who could possibly live in such an awful place. I am tired and hungry from our journey, please don't tease me."

The prince laughed, but instead of directly answering her question, said, "You can wash yourself and your clothes before you go in, if you like."

Glad of any excuse to put off climbing down into a dark, muddy hole, Abena removed her dress and started to wash it in the river. While her back was turned, the prince turned into a python again, and quickly climbed the tree above her. Abena looked around for her husband and, not seeing him, turned back to the task at hand. As she bent over the water, the python spat on her from the branch on which he rested. The spit landed in the middle of her back, and she whirled around. This time she saw her husband, the prince, sitting on a branch above her.

"Did you spit at me?" she asked, angrily shaking her fist.

The prince laughed. "Of course," he said. Then, climbing down the tree, he added, "Now get in the hole."

"No," said Abena, with all of her old arrogance.

"Very well, then," he said ominously, "if that's the way you want it." Almost immediately, Abena felt strange shivers coursing over her body. She held up her hands, and saw them shrink and wrinkle before her eyes. She leaned forward to look in the water, and saw the face of an ancient old crone staring back at her. She felt as though she were dying, and she quivered as she spoke, "Please, my husband, I beg of you, don't do this to me. I will do whatever you say, anything at all, just give me back my youth and beauty."

The prince spat again and Abena returned to the way she had been, but she no longer dared to disobey him so, weeping and moaning, she crawled into the hole.

And so their life together began. Every day the python, who no longer bothered to turn himself into a prince, would leave, saying to her "Abena, I am going hunting to get some food for us. Now, don't you dare move from this hole, or you know what I'll do to you!"

Time went by like this, and Abena never dared leave the hole. Her parents grew thin and old with worry, wondering why the maids had never returned, and why they never heard from their daughter.

A little bird used to come sit on a bush at the edge of Abena's old village, near where the children played, and sing this song:

Abena listened not to advice

Abena was too good for advice

Abena who's full of trouble

Abena is in big trouble

Abena who's full of trouble

Abena is in big trouble

The children sang the song in front of their parents, who at first took no notice. But finally someone remembered Abena, and her reputation for difficult behavior, and went to see her parents. He said, "There is a little bird who sings:

Abena listened not to advice

Abena was too good for advice

Abena who's full of trouble

Abena is in big trouble

Abena who's full of trouble

Abena is in big trouble

I WAS NEVER HERE...

Do you think it might be talking about your Abena?" Well, the parents were sure of it, but they had no idea how to find their daughter. This only added to their worries, and soon Abena's mother, who hadn't been able to eat since she heard about the song, fell ill and died. The father, now totally alone in the world, followed shortly behind her.

The little bird then left the village and went to the river where Abena lived in her hole. He sat on a twig by the tree under which she and her husband lived, and every day he sang:

> Abena, poor miserable wretch Abena
>
> Her mother is dead, Abena
>
> Her father is dead, Abena
>
> And she's in blissful ignorance, Abena

Each day, Abena listened to the song and wondered what it could mean. After a few days, she located the source, and would poke her head out of the hole as soon as her husband left for the day, and watch the bird.

One day she said to him timidly, "Little bird, is it me you are singing about?" The bird hopped down near her face and, putting his head to one side, replied, "Abena, poor miserable wretch Abena. Indeed, my song is about you." And Abena wept bitterly.

Finally, through her tears, she begged the bird, "Little bird, I beg of you to go to my village and tell my people where I am. I would return on my own, even though I have no more family, but the road is long and I can no longer find my way. And anyway, my husband, the python, would catch me before I had gone very far. Indeed, he may catch you. Go quickly, before he returns."

The little bird flew away, and by he evening he had come to the village. This time he bypassed the outskirts, and settled in a tree in the middle of the square to sing his song:

> Abena, poor miserable wretch Abena

Her mother is dead, Abena
Her father is dead, Abena
And she sits in a hole by the river, Abena

A small crowd soon gathered around the tree and, when the bird thought there were enough people, he stopped repeating that little verse, and went on to tell the story of what had happened to Abena. As the tale unfolded, the villagers grew angry, and those whose daughters had left as maids wept bitterly when they heard their children had been eaten. Soon all the village was ready to seek revenge upon the python.

The young men, many of whom had once courted Abena, collected their knives and guns and, led by the most fearless hunter—whom Abena had once mocked as a mere bushman unworthy of her love— they asked the bird to show them the way to the river. They traveled under cover of darkness, and by the second night they had reached the spot.

"Hide here," the bird cautioned them. "When the python comes out of his hole in the morning, I will sing, and then you can catch him before he goes hunting."

So the hunters laid in wait and soon the python awoke. He warned Abena not to leave, as usual, and then crawled up out of the hole.

There he is

sang the bird, and the hunters rushed out from their spot, ambushing him. Guns cracked and knives flashed, and soon the python was no more.

The hunters called to Abena, and thin and sickly-looking, she climbed out of the hole and lay weeping on the river bank. No one had the heart to scold her, so they carried her back to the village. Her family hut no longer existed, and she had to go live with cousins.

As soon as she was strong enough, she called all the young girls to her and sang them this song.

> Listen when your mother speaks
> Listen when your mother speaks
> For mothers know it all.
> If only I had listened to mother
> My life would have been so much better.

As long as she lived, Abena devoted herself to being a good aunty, helping to bring up the village's young girls. Every evening, she would gather them around her, and they would all sing Abena's Song, as it came to be known:

> Listen when your mother speaks
> For mothers know it all . . .

✕✕ **VEAL PRINCESS CORDON BLEU** ✕✕

*Living in Australia, I cook not only elaborate French meals and African
specialties, but all sorts of other foods as well. So, I'm giving you the recipe for
my Veal Cordon Bleu Dorinda Style, in addition to a couple of tasty
African dishes that I like to make at home for my children.*

SERVES 4

8 lean veal cutlets

$^1/_4$ cup (2 oz/60 g) butter or margarine

$^1/_4$ cup (2 fl oz/60 ml) corn or safflower oil

$^1/_4$ cup (2 fl oz/60 ml) brandy

2 chicken stock cubes

I pint (20 fl oz/600 ml) heavy cream (or a mixture
    of one-half cream and one-half plain yogurt,
    beaten together)

Freshly ground black pepper

Pinch of garlic powder (optional)

I pound ($^1/_2$ kg) button mushrooms

Flatten the veal cutlets with a steak mallet (if you buy your meat
from a butcher, you can ask to have this done at the shop.)

Combine the butter (or margarine) and oil in a heavy skillet and heat
until the butter has melted and the mixture is hot. Fry the cutlets several at a time, turning to cook both sides, just until they lose their pink
color. Do not overcook. Keep cooked veal warm in a medium hot oven
(330°F / 150°C) as you cook successive batches of veal.

When all of the meat is cooked, pour off any excess fat from the pan
and return all of the cutlets to the pan and toss well to ensure even tem-
perature, then lower the heat to medium low.

Add the brandy to the pan, strike a match, and ignite the fumes.
Carefully stir the meat until the flames die down (about 15–20 seconds).
Then crush the stock cubes and sprinkle them all over the meat.

Add the cream, lots of freshly ground black pepper, garlic powder (if
desired) and mushrooms. Stir well to mix and simmer on low heat until
the meat is tender and the sauce thickened. Serve hot.

　　　　　　　　　　　　　　　I WAS NEVER HERE...

✕✕ **PEANUT SOUP WITH CHICKEN** ✕✕

SERVES 4

2 pounds (1 kg) chicken, in pieces (should be
   about 6–8 pieces)
Salt and pepper to taste
2 large onions, finely chopped
13 oz (400 g) canned tomatoes
Heaping $^3/_4$ cup (6$^1/_2$ oz/200 g) peanut butter
3$^1/_2$ pints (2 L) boiling water
2–3 small red chile peppers, seeded and finely
   chopped
4–8 mushrooms
2 pounds (1 kg) precooked fish fillets (can be salted,
   smoked, grilled, deep-fried, or dried)

Season the chicken with salt and pepper, and place in a very large, heavy saucepan. Add the chopped onions and cook together on medium heat, stirring continuously, until the outside of the meat is "sealed," or slightly cooked.

Blend the canned tomatoes to a smooth consistency, then pour into the meat and onion mixture. Stir, and allow to simmer.

In a large bowl, combine the peanut butter and 1½ cups (500 ml) of the boiling water. With a wooden spoon, blend together until the mixture is a creamy, smooth sauce. (This can also be done in a blender or food processor.) Add to the meat and tomato mixture along with the chiles and mushrooms. Mix well, then stir in the rest of the water and the cooked fish, and simmer for an additional 30 minutes on medium heat, until the chicken is fully cooked and the soup somewhat thickened and reduced.

Serve hot over fufu (see page 37).

※※ BAKED PLANTAIN LOAF ※※

SERVES 4

2 large plantains, very ripe
2 teaspoons (10 g) fresh Shitor (see recipe, pg. 53)
1 cup (8 oz/250 g) brown rice flour
Salt to taste
2 tablespoons (2 fl oz/60 ml) corn oil
2 teaspoons (10 g) turmeric powder

Peel the plantains, cut them into small chunks, and place them in a large, deep mixing bowl. Mash into a thick paste using your fingers or a wooden spoon, or blend the whole lot in a blender or food processor, in which case you may need to add a tablespoon or two of water for smoother blending. Add the shitor, rice flour, and salt, and blend together thoroughly.

Gently heat the corn oil in a frying pan, then add the turmeric. Stir well, then remove mixture from heat and blend it into the plantain mixture. The resulting batter should be thick, yet easy to pour. If it is too runny, add rice flour a teaspoon at a time; if too stiff, add small amounts of water until it reaches the desired consistency.

Pour the mixture into a greased loaf pan and bake at 325 ° F (165° C) for one hour, or until firm and cooked throughout.

Let stand 5–10 minutes after removing from oven, then turn onto a wire rack to cool. Slice and serve as a light meal with salted peanuts, or as an accompaniment to stews or soups. Note: To slice this loaf easily, use a sharp bread knife that's been dipped in boiling water.

Let the Dancing Do the Talking!

My daughter Nuala is a fabulous dancer, always has been. Indeed, she's been studying dance virtually all her life, and performing since she was four. Now, as you know from your reading of my life, I too have always loved performing, but there was something about the way the Australian dance schools handled it that seemed unhealthy to me. Children were expected not just to perform in annual recitals, but to compete with their peers in fairly stressful exhibitions.

I had always known that my daughter was an above-average dancer, but I didn't think it was necessary for her to submit herself for approval—on stage or anywhere else! Still, participating in these competitions was the expected thing, and as long as I can recall, she has done so not just willingly, but even, at times, joyfully. It is fun, after all, to perform on stage, to hear the applause, and to work on routines with your dance-school friends. Still, not every competition taught the right lessons.

These week-long events involved a number of different factors—solos, duets, trios, quartets, quintets, groups, ballet, jazz, tap, folk, international—but the highlight was always the chance for individual schools of dance to compete against each other. The judges were often outside professionals of some repute, and prizes were awarded for each category as the competition progressed toward the final showdown between schools.

Now, despite my earlier comment that these things don't seem totally healthy, I have to say that a spirit of fun often reigned over all. Aptitude, proficiency, originality, and innovation were being celebrated, and kids do love to dress up and show off. Backstage, there was always an air of excitement and anticipation as competitors compared costumes or helped each other into particularly elaborate get-ups, parents and teachers made last-minute costume and make-up adjustments, and the mean kids teased anyone less fortunate than themselves. Even without teasing, the pressure was immense, and it was a wonder if some poor kid didn't throw up, burst into tears, or refuse to go on stage at least once per year. And that's just the kids! Now, about the mothers....

I think it's fair to say that every mother thinks her child is gifted in some way or another. The only difference is that most mothers are too modest to jump up and down and make a lot of noise about it. These dance competitions were a perfect showcase for those driven mothers who weren't too modest—and I am pleased to say that I was never one of them. Don't get me wrong, I loved to watch my daughter dance and was pleased to support her all the way. And, like her mother, Nuala always seems to put on her best shows under pressure, so I could be pretty sure she'd be good for a superior performance. Still, quietly confident though I might have been, I was also very much aware that, as her mother, I might be just a trifle biased. Also, more seriously, I was always mindful of the fact that we were living at a time—and in a country—where there is often some sort of problem giving *any* accolades to black people, however well deserved.

The competition in question happened when Nuala was about

seven. For her solo, she had chosen the *chapenakis,* a Mexican folk dance. I had helped her with her costume and hair, and her brother and father and I had watched her practice it so many times that we could all probably have performed it ourselves, if not as gracefully. There were a lot of competitors in her section, and she appeared about halfway down the roster. When her number was finally announced, I took a deep breath and stayed still, trying hard not to hear my own heartbeat. I found myself stroking her brother's hand—although whether to reassure him or myself, I'm still not sure.

Nuala danced exquisitely. My heart went out to this brave little girl, the only black child in her section and one of only a few black kids in the whole dance competitions. Her interpretation of the music and the dance was flawless. I was confident she would be rewarded for her efforts today, for once. I breathed a sigh of relief when it was o'er, and relaxed to enjoy the other children who followed; Nuala joined us in the audience to applaud her friends. When the section finally finished, there was the usual clapping and hubbub of noise until the judge slapped down her gavel for silence so she could announce the winners.

The honorable mention winner was announced, then the third place. Each child stepped forward to shake the judge's hand and collect their prize. Then the second place winner, and finally the first. Nuala's name was not among them. I hid my hurt for her sake as she dropped her head forward and stared down at the floor. I knew she was fighting back tears.

As the first-prize winner made to leave the stage, the audience broke into a deliberate, slow but regular clapping, the sort one uses to register a protest. They obviously did not agree with the judge's choice for first place, but I had no idea that their protest was in support of my daughter. At least not until I received the assessment sheet given out to each contestant at the end of each day.

My beautiful daughter's evaluation read:

Parents should refrain from applying such heavy body make-up on the children in order for them to look the part. This contestant's make-up was far too heavy even for a Mexican! Too much emphasis was placed on appearance. It is something to note for future performances.

She did not mention the child's dance abilities at all.

I was livid. Not only did her comments have no bearing whatsoever on Nuala's talent, but, of course, the child had worn no body make-up at all. She didn't need to.

Clutching the assessment sheet in my hand, I marched up to the judge, stuck it under her nose, and demanded to know whether she had written the piece of nonsense on the sheet. Arrogantly, she confirmed she had. I insisted she take a good look at my face so as never to forget it, then proceeded to dress her down properly. I started with what must have been obvious to everyone but her: the fact that the child had danced brilliantly, and pointed out what I had by then figured out, which is that even the audience had registered a protest. Secondly, I told her, a crab can only produce another crab or variations thereof, and certainly not a bird. Or, in other words, it's not my fault that my child wasn't born white, and I could not believe that she was penalizing a child of mixed parentage for being born already tanned!

I gave her a number of choices: she could either recall all the dancers and review the entire section again, rejudge based on her notes and announce her new choices over the loudspeaker, or do nothing, in which case I would go onstage and tell the audience what she had written about my daughter. She chose to re-jig her choices, and when she took up the microphone, she announced that Nuala had won a joint honorable mention. It was not good enough.

The mother whose daughter won first prize came to me and said,

"I really do know who should have won, and I feel bad that my daughter got the prize. I know in my heart of hearts that this trophy really belongs to your daughter. Please take it."

I declined, not wanting to hurt the other girl, but thanked her for her honesty. Nuala, of course, was horribly embarrassed, and relieved when I finally backed down. She has always felt that my protests and defenses of her rights were futile and, with the natural conservatism of children, wishes I would just stop making such a fuss.

Now, I have always believed that every ocean is made of little drops, and that every little protest is some help against the greater evil of discrimination. My children don't always agree. They have often felt that prejudice is too deeply ingrained in our society for my little efforts to make any difference at all. Part of this, I think, has to do with having grown up in Australia, where they will never be accepted as natives. Their experience is so different from my supportive Ghanaian childhood—everywhere they go, they are confronted by people who insist they must be foreign. Of course, they are my children, so they're likely to come back with the retort that, with the exception of the aborigines, they weren't aware of anyone on Australia who *didn't*, according to what they'd learned in history, come from somewhere else.

But it wears you down. We love Australia, and consider ourselves Australian. My children may have been born in London to Ghanaian-British parents, but they've lived down under since they were one and two years old. They have visited my family in Ghana, and their father's in Britain, but only as tourists. This is home. So where do they go when people tell them to go back where they came from? And how do we react when Nuala wins a dance contest, as she has many times since that one awful day, and people congratulate us by saying, "Well, you'd never get this in the jungle, would you?"

It is at times like this that I have to ask myself, Am I really here and are these things really happening to me? I never planned it like this.

Still, I believe that things work out for the best. I am slowly, drop by drop, raising consciousness here in Australia, and even around the world, about my African culture. And my daughter is free to pick a career in dance, or performance, or anything else she wants, a freedom I never had. I often feel like a pioneer, laying down the foundations and breaking prejudices in the hopes that by the time my daughter gets to where I am, the whole scenery will be different. Then I will know that I *was* here, and this *did* happen, and I have prevailed.

BRAVE KAANIWA YAA

A long time ago in a big Ashanti village, there lived a wonderful woman whose name was Kaaniwa Yaa. Kaaniwa Yaa was old, but she was hardworking, and she owned a big farm about five miles outside the village. She tended to this farm on her own. There she grew plentiful yams, plantains, onions, tomatoes, cassava, chiles—indeed, every kind of food you can imagine.

Well, every day she would set off for her farm, striding easily and humming happily to herself as she went. Once there, she would work all day, digging, weeding, planting, and harvesting whatever produce was ripe to bring back home. Because, you see, Kaaniwa Yaa had a lot of mouths to feed, for living in the same house with her were her sixteen grandchildren. Yes, sixteen grandchildren, from her many daughters and sons, as well as five more children who belonged to her two tenants. But Kaaniwa Yaa loved having all these children around and it pleased her to feed them with the fruits of her labor.

One day when she went as usual to her farm, she found that half of her crop had been stolen. Huge bunches of plantain, bananas, yams, onions, tomatoes, chiles, and cassava were missing.

"Who could have done such a thing?" said the old woman out loud, although there was no one around to hear her. "How selfish, how mean. It must be a thief. It couldn't have been my grandchildren. Or maybe it's the tenants. Yes, it must be the tenants."

And so she hurried to the tenants house, eager to accuse them and solve the mystery for once and for all. But the tenants denied everything, so she asked her grandchildren if they had committed the awful act. They, too, said no.

Turning to her oldest granddaughter, the old woman said, "Ama Serwah, it must be you who is stealing from me, I saw you giving something away this morning before I left. I am sure it was bunches of plantain from my farm."

"But Grandmother, you told us not to eat food given to us by strangers. Somebody gave me some bananas yesterday and some plantain today, so I only gave them to the beggars who come to the front gate. They didn't come from your farm."

Kaaniwa took no notice of her granddaughter's explanation. She was consumed with rage. She threw her tenants out of her house and she threw out all of her grandchildren until such time as they learned not to steal from her. Even though they weren't guilty, the poor little kids had to go live with their respective parents in overcrowded homes and the tenants had to find new lodgings. All except Ama Serwah, who decided she would just leave the town altogether and go to find work in another village.

Within the week, word reached Kaaniwa that other farmers in the area were also having food stolen. They had tried everything to catch the thief; they set traps, they sent out search parties, but their efforts were in vain.

Frustrated, the farmers went to the Chief. After all, they paid their taxes and they deserved protection! But the Chief's men were also unsuccessful in catching the thief. Several times they came close to apprehending him, but somehow he always managed to slay his pursuers. The few survivors ran back to the Chief, terrorized, and refused to go out after the thief again.

As time went on, the thief grew bolder. Soon, not only was produce being stolen—children were disappearing, and men and women reported being attacked when they tried to fetch water from the outskirts of the village. This thief was wreaking havoc on everyone's lives.

One day, just when the villagers were beside themselves with worry, two men who had gone to collect firewood came rushing in, saying, "Ama Serwah, Kaaniwa Yaa's granddaughter, has been killed. We think it was done by the devil incarnate himself—he looks like a beggar, a huge beggar. He has killed Ama Serwah, we know he killed her because we saw him carrying her waist cloth and her sandals!"

Well, the old lady was distraught when she heard this, she cried and cried and cried. She asked the Chief if she could find this beggar, this killer, this thief, and bring him back for punishment.

But the Chief said, "No, you are only a woman, you can't do that, I will send the army out after him."

So the chief sent his army of men, divided them into two groups, and for a whole week they searched, but they couldn't find the thief.

The old lady was inconsolable. Finally she made her decision. The Chief had said that nobody was to go very far outside the village without the army's protection, but Kaaniwa took no notice, she just had to go and find her granddaughter. How guilty she felt for accusing the poor child of stealing from her. What was a little food, now that her favorite granddaughter had been killed? Kaaniwa swore that if nothing else, she would find her granddaughter's body and bring it back for a noble burial.

She picked up a calabash, and caught three chickens from her backyard. Then she packed a bag of cola nuts soaked in herbs in a rag and set off on her journey. She walked and walked, far beyond her farm, and then she turned southwards. Soon she came upon a river where she saw some children playing in the water, and people washing their laundry.

Suddenly, she heard a familiar laugh and she called out, "Ama Serwah, is that you?"

And the voice answered, "Yes, I am Ama Serwah, but who is calling me?"

"I am your grandmother, Kaaniwa Yaa. But what happened to you? I heard in the village that you were dead."

"Oh no, Grandma. I went from village to village when you threw us out, looking for work. These kind villagers took me in and said if I could help them do their laundry they would give me food and shelter and pay me a small wage at the end of each week."

"So what happened to your cloth then?"

"Well, you see, I came upon a huge beggar, and he tried to catch me, but I ran as fast as I could to get away. As I was escaping, my clothes caught on some thorns, and I figured that if I took my sandals off, I could run much faster. When I finally found this village, I had only my top on, but they were kind and took me in."

Kaaniwa Yaa said, "My dear granddaughter, I am so sorry I mistrusted you and I am so happy to see you alive. But now I must continue on my journey. I must find this wicked nasty man and bring him to justice."

Ama Serwah didn't want her grandmother to go, but she knew she couldn't stop the determined old lady. That very same day, Kaaniwa Yaa walked slowly back to her farm. There she set about building a little hut, very carefully, and then she picked from her own farm little bits of food, which she cooked in the little pot she had brought with her. After she ate, she set about making a little bed inside the hut she had built and, using that old raggedy cloth she'd brought with her, she made a little pillow and lay down to sleep.

Just as nighttime fell, she heard noises in the field, so she got up and slowly crept to the door. There she saw a man, a big tall filthy man with a bushy beard, and he was digging up the food from her farm.

He was pretty scary-looking, but Kaaniwa Yaa was not impressed. She was a feisty brave old thing. She came out and said, "What do you think you are doing?"

The man looked at her and picked up his gun, ready to shoot; in his other hand he had a big knife, which he'd been using to dig up the food with. He was on the attack until he got closer and had a better look at her. "Oh it's just an old lady," he said. "What are you doing out here in the woods at this hour of night? Go back to sleep before I do you in."

Kaaniwa Yaa said, "I am a beggar, a poor beggar. I am an outcast and I have nowhere to go. Can you help me?"

"What do you want me to do?"

"Well, it looks like you have got plenty of food here, and I know where you can find big yams. Let me show you where you can dig up the big ones, so we can cook."

The man was amused with this dear old beggar, so he took her with him and together they dug up the best yams from the old lady's own farm. The thief took her to his secret hideout and, in a way, they became friends. This then went on for many, many weeks. She would go back with him to her own farm, where she would help him steal her own produce and eat her own chickens. The thief took a real liking to her, and he looked after her.

One day, the old lady decided she had to get her own back on this man. Just after dinner, she suggested that they chew some cola nuts. Now, she had cleverly brought along with her some nuts that had not been soaked in the dangerous herbs, so she started chewing those and offered to her friend the nasty nuts. He took them and chewed them and soon he was in a deep, deep, deep sleep. As soon as he slept, the old lady tied him up with a rope; she tied his arms and his legs behind him so that he couldn't move. She pulled as tightly as her strength could manage and she tied him to a tree.

That done, she ran as fast as she could to the village where her granddaughter Ama Serwah was staying. Kaaniwa Yaa told them what she had done with that murderer, so they sent a whole party to her village so that the Chief's army could fetch the thief.

When the army brought the thief in, everybody was astounded. How did such a feeble old lady manage to capture such a strong tyrant? The secret was to remain with the old woman until the day she died. But this incredible feat did not escape the Chief's attention. A new post was created amongst the ruling elders specifically for the woman; Kaaniwa Yaa took her position with pride, and her bravery went down in history.

Why the Black Woman Smiles

I cannot tell you how many times people have come up to me and, in a misguided attempt at conversation, said something like "your people always look so happy" or "black people are always smiling, they look so happy." Excuse me? Given all the history that they *know* exists between the races, I am astounded that white people really believe that the whole black race is so happy that we just can't help smiling all day.

Yes, it's true that the black woman uses her smile when she's happy, but that's just the beginning of the story. All too often, black women have far less reason to smile than their white counterparts, but, nonetheless they do so. To the black woman, a smile doesn't just register an emotion. No, the smile is a secret weapon stored deep within her in some unreachable private place. Each smile holds a story, in a language of its own.

Over the years, I have observed black women break out in rueful smiles when surveying the wreckage of a year's crops burnt in a bush fire. I've seen them smile with resignation at the sight of a sick child whose treatment they can't afford, smirk at their reflections in the mirror, saying, "So he left you for a younger woman, huh?" And then there is the smile that says, "I didn't understand a word of what you said but it's fine 'cause I've withdrawn to my secret comfortable place, so keep talking!" The black woman smiles in disbelief, and through her tears, pain, humiliation, and love. Her smile is at once a mask to hide behind and a shield to protect against the pain of survival. It is very likely incomprehensible to anyone who hasn't lived it.

I find comfort in the knowledge that I am not alone when I smile. In Africa, the women would understand my smiles, because they wear the same ones. In my performance work, I always search the faces of my audiences, hoping that my smiles will recognize others in an embrace of common humanity. And I wonder if the language of smiles can be passed on to our children or whether it must be acquired through life's school of hard knocks.

When I arrived in England, it was important to me to be hip, and the hippest thing to do was to shed my blackness. I wanted to be accepted, to blend in. I straightened my hair, wore make-up, and packed away my Ghanaian fabrics and clothes to be replaced by jeans, dresses, blouses, and skirts. I accessorized. And of course, the most important accessory is one's attitude, one's mannerisms and accent. So for years I stopped smiling. It seemed too ethnic, and anyway, the locals didn't smile much, so why should I? The whole process was so insidious that I lost track of what was going on. It seemed natural, like acclimatization. I only became conscious of it again later; much later.

Times may have changed since then, but human behavior hasn't. The children we've since had overseas are emulating our old ways; they have taken on the respective local mantles of "No smiles please, we're foreign." It is said in Ghana that wherever you bury a baby's umbilical cord is where they will ultimately finish up; like many of African descent, my umbilical cord was buried in the soil of my homeland. Where do we bury those of our children? This dilemma is what consistently wipes the collective smiles off our black faces. How do we resolve it, other than being there when they need us, ready with a big heart and a smile?

I have often been asked what I miss most about Africa, and the answer is invariably the same: I miss the irreverent humor of African women, their ability to really have a good laugh together. They share in-jokes about their men, their families, their lives. They have this wonderful self-deprecatory humor; in the face of adversity, they laugh medicinally. Jamaican patois describes this tendency as "tek bad ting mek joke!" This ability to laugh is part of the residual baggage I've retained from Ghana. I've been happy to carry it with me because it serves me so well. It is my secret tonic.

It's been a long trip and I think that however else others see me now, I will always be that little Glenda Miller with a dream, dancing for her mother's patients in Ashanti New Town. I've come, I've seen, I've not quite conquered yet, but I'm in there for the long haul.

Every so often though, I have to stop long enough to pinch myself and ask, Am I really here and are these things actually happening? One thing I'm sure of, whatever happens, I will continue to smile.

I am here.

✕✕